BENCHMARK SERIES

Microsoft®

Word

2016
Level 2

Workbook

Rutkosky • Roggenkamp • Rutkosky

PARADIGM
EDUCATION SOLUTIONS

St. Paul

Senior Vice President	Linda Hein
Editor in Chief	Christine Hurney
Director of Production	Timothy W. Larson
Production Editor	Jen Weaverling
Cover and Text Designer	Valerie King
Copy Editors	Communicáto, Ltd.
Senior Design and Production Specialist	Jack Ross
Design and Production Specialist	PerfecType
Assistant Developmental Editors	Mamie Clark, Katie Werdick
Testers	Janet Blum, Fanshawe College; Traci Post
Instructional Support Writers	Janet Blum, Fanshawe College; Brienna McWade
Indexer	Terry Casey
Vice President Information Technology	Chuck Bratton
Digital Projects Manager	Tom Modl
Vice President Sales and Marketing	Scott Burns
Director of Marketing	Lara Weber McLellan

Trademarks: Microsoft is a trademark or registered trademark of Microsoft Corporation in the United States and/or other countries. Some of the product names and company names included in this book have been used for identification purposes only and may be trademarks or registered trade names of their respective manufacturers and sellers. The authors, editors, and publisher disclaim any affiliation, association, or connection with, or sponsorship or endorsement by, such owners.

We have made every effort to trace the ownership of all copyrighted material and to secure permission from copyright holders. In the event of any question arising as to the use of any material, we will be pleased to make the necessary corrections in future printings.

Cover Photo Credits: © Photomall/Dreamstime.com

Paradigm Publishing is independent from Microsoft Corporation, and not affiliated with Microsoft in any manner. While this publication may be used in assisting individuals to prepare for a Microsoft Office Specialist certification exam, Microsoft, its designated program administrator, and Paradigm Publishing do not warrant that use of this publication will ensure passing a Microsoft Office Specialist certification exam.

ISBN 978-0-76386-924-3 (digital)
ISBN 978-0-76387-158-1 (print)

© 2017 by Paradigm Publishing, Inc.
875 Montreal Way
St. Paul, MN 55102
Email: educate@emcp.com
Website: ParadigmCollege.com

Printed in the United States of America

24 23 22 21 20 19 18 17 16   3 4 5 6 7 8 9 10 11 12

Contents

WORD 2016

Microsoft® Word Level 2

Unit 1

Formatting and Customizing Documents

> SNAP

Study Tools

Study tools include a presentation and a list of chapter Quick Steps and Hint margin notes. Use these resources to help you further develop and review skills learned in this chapter.

Concepts Check

Check your understanding by identifying application tools used in this chapter. If you are a SNAP user, launch the Concepts Check from your Assignments page.

Recheck

Check your understanding by taking this quiz. If you are a SNAP user, launch the Recheck from your Assignments page.

Skills Exercise

Additional activities are available to SNAP users. If you are a SNAP user, access these activities from your Assignments page.

Skills Assessment

Assessment

1

Data Files

Define and Apply Custom Bullets and Multilevel Lists to a Technology Document

1. Open **TechTimeline.docx** and then save it with the name **1-TechTimeline**.
2. Select the questions below the heading *Technology Information Questions* and then insert check mark (✓) bullets.
3. Define a cell phone symbol ()bullet in 14-point font size and then apply the symbol bullet to the 11 paragraphs of text below the heading *Technology Timeline: Personal Communications Technology*. (To find the cell phone symbol, display the Webdings font at the Symbol dialog box and then type 200 in the *Character code* text box.)
4. Select the paragraphs of text below the heading *Information Systems and Commerce*, click the Multilevel List button, and then click the middle option in the top row of the *List Library* section.
5. Select the paragraphs of text below the heading *Internet* and then apply the same multilevel list numbering.
6. Save and then print page 3 of **1-TechTimeline.docx**.
7. Select the paragraphs of text below the heading *Information Systems and Commerce* and then define a new multilevel list with the following specifications:
   a. Level 1 inserts arabic numbers (1, 2, 3), each followed by a period. The numbers are aligned at the left margin (at 0 inch) with the text indent at 0.25 inch.
   b. Level 2 inserts capital letters (A, B, C), each followed by a period. The letters are aligned at 0.25 inch from the left margin with the text indent at 0.5 inch.

c. Level 3 inserts arabic numbers (1, 2, 3), each followed by a right parenthesis. The numbers are aligned at 0.5 inch from the left margin with the text indent at 0.75 inch.

d. Make sure the new multilevel list numbering is applied to the selected paragraphs.

8. Select the paragraphs of text below the heading *Internet* and then apply the new multilevel list numbering.

9. Insert a header that prints the page number at the right margin on each page *except* the first page.

10. Insert the text *Cell phones* and *Apple Pay* in text boxes as shown in Figure WB-1.1 with the following specifications:

a. Insert a text box below the arrow line near the bottom of page 1 and then type Cell phones in the text box.

b. Use the Text Direction button to rotate the text in the text box 270 degrees.

c. Remove the outline from the text box. **Hint: Do this with the Shape Outline button in the Shape Styles group**.

d. Change the text wrapping to *Behind Text*.

e. Drag the text box so it is positioned as shown in Figure WB-1.1.

f. Complete similar steps to create the text box with the text *Apple Pay* and position the text box as shown in the figure.

11. Move the insertion point to the right of the text *Electronic Commerce* (item 2) located on page 2 and then insert the image shown in Figure WB-1.2 with the following specifications:

a. Display the Insert Picture dialog box, navigate to the WL2C1 folder on your storage medium, and then double-click the **CreditCard.png** file.

b. Change the height of the image to 1.8 inches.

c. Apply shadow and glow effects of your choosing to the image.

d. Apply the Paint Strokes artistic effect (second column, second row in the Artistic Effects button drop-down gallery).

e. Apply Tight text wrapping.

f. Precisely position the image on the second page with an absolute horizontal measurement of 4.5 inches from the right edge of the page and an absolute vertical measurement of 4.3 inches below the top of the page.

g. Compress the image. (Use the Compress Pictures button in the Adjust group on the Picture Tools Format tab.)

12. Save, print, and then close **1-TechTimeline.docx**.

Figure WB-1.1 Assessment 1, Step 10

Figure WB-1.2 Assessment 1, Step 11

Information Systems and Commerce

1. Information Systems
   A. Information System Classifications
      1) Distribution Management Systems
      2) Office Information Systems
      3) Management Information Systems
      4) Decision Support Systems
      5) Executive Support Systems
   B. Choosing an Information System
      1) User Interface Design
      2) Niche Information Systems
      3) Turnkey Solutions
      4) System Support
2. Electronic Commerce
   A. Transaction Payment Methods
      1) Check or Credit Card by Phone
      2) Credit Accounts
      3) Credit Cards
      4) Smart Cards
      5) Digital Cash
      6) Electronic Wallets
      7) Apple Pay
   B. Business-to-Business Software
      1) Electronic Data Exchange
      2) Payment and Transaction Systems
      3) Security Technologies
      4) Customer Relationship Management

Assessment 2

Data Files

Insert Specialized Footers in a Report

1. Open **Robots.docx** and then save it with the name **1-Robots**.
2. Make the following changes to the document:
   a. Apply the Heading 2 style to the title *ROBOTS AS ANDROIDS*.
   b. Apply the Heading 3 style to the headings *Visual Perception*, *Audio Perception*, *Tactile Perception*, *Locomotion*, and *Navigation*.
   c. Apply the Lines (Distinctive) style set.
   d. Change the paragraph spacing to Relaxed. (Use the Paragraph Spacing button in the Document Formatting group on the Design tab.)
   e. Center the title *ROBOTS AS ANDROIDS*.
   f. Keep the heading *Navigation* together with the paragraph of text that follows it.
3. Create an odd page footer that includes the following:
   a. Insert the current date at the left margin. (Choose the date option that displays the month spelled out, such as *January 1, 2018*.)
   b. Using the Pictures button in the Insert group on the Header & Footer Tools Design tab, insert the **Robot.png** image in the middle of the footer. Change the height of the robot image to 0.5 inches and the text wrapping to Behind Text. Drag the robot image down below the footer pane border.
   c. At the right margin, type Page, press the spacebar, and then insert a page number at the current position.
4. Create an even page footer that includes the following:
   a. At the left margin, type Page, press the spacebar, and then insert a page number at the current position.
   b. Insert the **Robot.png** image in the middle of the footer and apply the same formatting as you did to the image in the odd page footer.
   c. Insert the current date at the right margin in the same format you chose for the odd page footer.
5. Save, print, and then close **1-Robots.docx**.

Assessment

3

Data Files

Insert a Section Break and Format and Print Sections

1. Open **CompViruses.docx** and then save it with the name **1-CompViruses**.
2. Insert a section break that begins a new page at the beginning of the title *CHAPTER 2: SECURITY RISKS*.
3. Move the insertion point to the beginning of the document and then create a footer for the first section in the document that prints *Chapter 1* at the left margin, the page number in the middle, and your first and last names at the right margin.
4. Edit the footer for the second section so it prints *Chapter 2* instead of *Chapter 1*. *Hint: Make sure you break the link.*
5. Print only the pages in section 2.
6. Save and then close **1-CompViruses.docx**.

Assessment

4

Data Files

Format a Shape and Edit Points and Wrap Points

1. Open **CedarMeadows.docx** and then save it with the name **1-CedarMeadows**.
2. Select the shape in the document, display the Format Shape task pane and then apply the following formatting:
   a. Apply the Bottom Spotlight - Accent 5 gradient fill (fifth column, fourth row).
   b. Apply the Inside Bottom shadow effect (second column, third row in the *Inner* section).
   c. Close the Format Shape task pane.
3. Display editing points around the shape and then adjust the points so they display in a manner similar to what is shown in Figure WB-1.3. (Click outside the shape after adjusting the editing points.)
4. Select the shape, display wrap points, and then adjust the wrap points so they display in a manner similar to what is shown in Figure WB-1.3. (Click outside the shape after adjusting the wrap points.)
5. Save, print, and then close **1-CedarMeadows.docx**.

Figure WB-1.3 Assessment 4

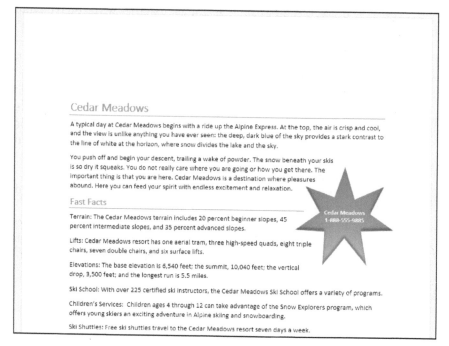

Assessment

5

Link Text Boxes

1. Open **ProtectIssues.docx** and then save it with the name **1-ProtectIssues**.
2. Select the text box at the left and link it to the text box at the right.
3. With the insertion point positioned in the text box at the left, insert the file named **ProIssues.docx**. (Use the Object button on the Insert tab.)
4. Adjust the columns so all of the text fits in the two columns by changing the width of both text boxes to 3.1 inches and the height of both to 8.4 inches.
5. Save, print, and then close **1-ProtectIssues.docx**.

Assessment

6

Insert a Horizontal Line in a Footer

1. Word includes a horizontal line feature that can be used to insert a graphic line in a document or a header or footer. Insert a horizontal line in a document by clicking the Borders button arrow in the Paragraph group on the Home tab and then clicking *Horizontal Line* at the drop-down list. Right-click the selected line type and then click *Picture* at the shortcut menu to display the Format Horizontal Line dialog box. Look at the formatting options that are available at the Format Horizontal Line dialog box and then click the Cancel button to close the dialog box.
2. Open **ShopOnline.docx** and then save it with the name **1-ShopOnline**.
3. Keep the heading *ONLINE SHOPPING MALLS* together with the paragraph that follows it.
4. Create a footer that contains a horizontal line in standard blue color (eighth color option in the *Standard Colors* section) with a height of 3 points.
5. Save, print, and then close **1-ShopOnline.docx**.

Visual Benchmark

Create and Format an International Correspondence Document

1. Open **IntlCorres.docx** and then save it with the name **1-IntlCorres**.
2. Apply the following formatting so your document appears similar to the document shown in Figure WB-1.4:

   - Change the top margin to 1.5 inches and the left and right margins to 1.25 inches.
   - Apply the Heading 1 style to the title and the Heading 2 style to the three headings.
   - Apply the Shaded style set. (You will need to click the More Style Sets button in the Document Formatting group to display this style set.)
   - Change the theme colors to Green.
   - Apply check mark bullets as shown in the figure.
   - Apply the symbol bullets as shown in the figure. (Find the globe bullet in the Webdings font, character code 254, at the Symbol dialog box.)
   - Apply automatic numbering as shown in the figure and start numbering with 11 after the heading *CANADIAN CODES AND TERRITORIES*.
   - Apply any other formatting required to make your document look similar to the document in the figure.
3. Save, print, and then close **1-IntlCorres.docx**.

INTERNATIONAL CORRESPONDENCE

With the increased number of firms conducting business worldwide, international written communication has assumed new importance. Follow these guidelines when corresponding internationally, especially with people for whom English is not the primary language:

- ✓ Use a direct writing style and clear, precise words.
- ✓ Avoid slang, jargon, and idioms.
- ✓ Develop an awareness of cultural differences that may interfere with the communication process.

INTERNATIONAL ADDRESSES

Use the company's letterhead or a business card as a guide for spelling and other information. Include the following when addressing international correspondence:

- Line 1: Addressee's Name, Title
- Line 2: Company Name
- Line 3: Street Address
- Line 4: City and Codes
- Line 5: COUNTRY NAME (capitalized)

CANADIAN CODES AND PROVINCES

1. ON – Ontario
2. QC – Quebec
3. NS – Nova Scotia
4. NB – New Brunswick
5. MB – Manitoba
6. BC – British Columbia
7. PE – Prince Edward Island
8. SK – Saskatchewan
9. AB – Alberta
10. NL – Newfoundland and Labrador

CANADIAN CODES AND TERRITORIES

11. NT – Northwest Territories
12. YT – Yukon
13. NU – Nunavut

Case Study

You work in the Human Resources Department at Oceanside Medical Services. Your supervisor, Michael Jennison, has given you a Word document containing employee handbook information and asked you to format the book. Open **OMSHandbook.docx**, save it with the name **1-OMSHandbook**, and then apply the following formatting:

- Apply heading styles to the titles and headings.
- Apply a style set of your choosing.
- Apply a theme that makes the handbook easy to read.
- Define a new symbol bullet and then apply it to all the currently bulleted paragraphs.
- Insert a section break that begins a new page at the beginning of each section heading (beginning with *Section 1: General Information*).
- Insert a footer that prints the section name at the left margin (except the first page) and page number at the right margin. Insert the correct section name for each section footer.

After reviewing the handbook, you decide to apply additional formatting to improve its readability and appearance. With **1-OMSHandbook.docx** open, apply the following formatting:

- Select the lines of text on the first page beginning with *Section 1: General Information* through *Compensation Procedures* and then define and apply a new multilevel list number format. That format should apply capital letters followed by periods to the first level and arabic numbers (1, 2, 3) followed by periods to the second level. You determine the indents.
- Insert a cover page of your choosing and insert the appropriate information in the placeholders.

Save, print, and then close **1-OMSHandbook.docx**.

An orientation for new employees at Oceanside Medical Services is scheduled for Friday, October 12, 2018, from 9:00 a.m. until 3:30 p.m. Michael Jennison will conduct the orientation and has asked you to prepare a flyer about it that can be placed on all at Oceanside Medical Services bulletin boards in the clinic. Include in the flyer the date and times of the orientation, as well as the location, which is Conference Room 100. Include as bullets additional information about what will be covered during the orientation. Use the information in the multilevel list in **1-OMSHandbook.docx** to produce six to eight bulleted points. Using the Help feature, learn how to insert a picture watermark and then insert the **Ocean.jpg** file as a watermark. Make sure the text in the flyer is readable. Include any other additional features to improve the appearance of the flyer. Save the completed flyer and name the document **1-OMSFlyer**. Print and then close the document.

During the Oceanside Medical Services new-employee orientation, Mr. Jennison will discuss vacation allowances and he wants to present the information in a readable format. He has asked you to look at the information in **OMSVacAllowances.docx** and then insert the information in tables. Apply formatting to make the tables attractive and the information easy to read. Save the completed document and name it **1-OMSVacAllowances**. Save, print, and then close the document.

Proofing Documents and Creating Charts

Study Tools

Study tools include a presentation and a list of chapter Quick Steps and Hint margin notes. Use these resources to help you further develop and review skills learned in this chapter.

Concepts Check

Check your understanding by identifying application tools used in this chapter. If you are a SNAP user, launch the Concepts Check from your Assignments page.

Recheck

Check your understanding by taking this quiz. If you are a SNAP user, launch the Recheck from your Assignments page.

Skills Exercise

Additional activities are available to SNAP users. If you are a SNAP user, access these activities from your Assignments page.

Skills Assessment

Assessment

1

Data Files

Check Spelling in a Punctuation Document

1. Open **QuoteMarks.docx** and then save it with the name **2-QuoteMarks**.
2. Complete a spelling and grammar check on the document.
3. Apply the Heading 1 style to the title of the document and the Heading 2 style to the headings in the document (which currently display in bold formatting).
4. Apply the Parallax theme.
5. Center the document title.
6. Save, print, and then close **2-QuoteMarks.docx**.

Assessment

2

Data Files

Check Spelling and Grammar and Proofread a Letter

1. Open **AirMiles.docx** and then save it with the name **2-AirMiles**.
2. Complete a spelling and grammar check on the document. (Proper names are spelled correctly.)
3. After completing the spelling and grammar check, proofread the letter and make any necessary changes. (The letter contains mistakes that the grammar checker will not select.) Replace the *XX* near the end of the document with your initials.
4. Select the entire document and then change the font to 12-point Candara.
5. Save, print, and then close **2-AirMiles.docx**.

Assessment 3

Check Spelling and Grammar and Display Readability Statistics and Word Count in a Document

1. Open **Ethics.docx** and then save it with the name **2-Ethics**.
2. Turn on the display of readability statistics and then complete a spelling and grammar check on the document. *41.2* *13.4*
3. Make a note of the Flesch Reading Ease score and the Flesch-Kindcaid Grade Level score and then type that information in the appropriate location toward the end of the document.
4. Turn off the display of readability statistics.
5. Determine the number of words in the document and then type that *370* information in the appropriate location toward the end of the document.
6. Apply formatting to enhance the appearance of the document. *font, style, theme etc.*
7. Save, print, and then close **2-Ethics.docx**.

put note of in bottom page.

Assessment 4

Translate and Insert Words in a Table

1. At a blank document, create a table and use the translation feature to find the Spanish and French translations of the following terms:

   abbreviation
   adjective
   adverb
   punctuation
   grammar
   hyphen
   paragraph

2. Type the English words in the first column of the table, the corresponding Spanish words in the second column, and the corresponding French words in the third column. (Do not include accents or special symbols.)
3. Apply formatting to enhance the appearance of the table.
4. Save the document and name it **2-Translations**.
5. Print and then close **2-Translations.docx**.

Assessment 5

Create and Format a Column Chart and Pie Chart

1. At a blank document, use the data in Figure WB-2.1 to create a column chart (using the default chart style at the Insert Chart dialog box) with the following specifications:
   a. Use the Chart Elements button outside the upper right border of the chart to add a data table and remove the legend.
   b. Apply the Style 4 chart style.
   c. Change the chart title to *Units Sold First Quarter*.
   d. Apply the Fill - Black, Text 1, Shadow WordArt style (first style) to the chart area.
   e. Change the chart height to 4 inches.
   f. Change the position of the chart to Position in Top Center with Square Text Wrapping.
2. Move the insertion point to the end of the document, press the Enter key two times, and then create a pie chart (using the default pie chart style at the Insert Chart dialog box) with the data shown in Figure WB-2.2 and with the following specifications:
   a. Apply the Style 3 chart style.
   b. Move the data labels to the inside end. ***Hint: Click the Chart Elements button, click the right-pointing arrow at the right side of*** Data Labels, ***and then click*** Inside End.

c. Change the chart title to *Expense Distribution*.

   d. Apply the Colored Outline - Orange, Accent 2 shape style to the title (third shape style).

   e. Change the chart height to 3 inches and the width to 5.5 inches.

   f. Change the position of the chart to Position in Bottom Center with Square Text Wrapping.

3. Save the document and name it **2-ColumnPieCharts**.

4. Print and then close **2-ColumnPieCharts.docx**.

Figure WB-2.1 Assessment 5, Data for Column Chart

Salesperson	January	February	March
Barnett	55	60	42
Carson	20	24	31
Fanning	15	30	13
Han	52	62	58
Mahoney	49	52	39

Figure WB-2.2 Assessment 5, Data for Pie Chart

Category	Percentage
Salaries	67%
Travel	15%
Equipment	11%
Supplies	7%

Visual Benchmark

Use the Translator Feature

Data Files

1. Open **CCDonations.docx** and then save it with the name **2-CCDonations**.

2. Type the paragraph of text below the heading *English:* as shown in Figure WB-2.3 and then complete a spelling and grammar check on the text.

3. Select the paragraph of text below the heading *English:* and then translate the paragraph into Spanish and then into French. Copy the translated text into the document as shown in Figure WB-2.3 (Your translations may vary slightly from those shown in the figure.)

4. Use the Curlz MT font to format the heading at the beginning of each paragraph and the quote that displays near the end of the letter. Apply paragraph shading as shown in the figure.

5. Save, print, and then close **2-CCDonations.docx**.

Figure WB-2.3 Visual Benchmark

Support Your Local Community Center

English:

As you consider your donation contributions for the coming year, we ask that you consider supporting your community by supporting the Cordova Children's Community Center. The center is a nonprofit agency providing educational and recreational activities for children. Please stop by for a visit. Our dedicated staff will be available to discuss with you the services offered by the center, how your donation dollars are spent, and provide information on current and future activities and services.

Spanish:

Considerar sus contribuciones de donación para el año que viene, te pedimos que considere apoyo a su comunidad mediante el apoyo a centro de comunidad de niños de Córdoba. El centro es una agencia sin fines de lucro que ofrece actividades educativas y recreativas para los niños. Favor de pasar por una visita. Nuestro personal estará disponible para discutir con usted los servicios ofrecidos por el centro, cómo se gastan sus dólares de donación y proporcionar información sobre las actividades actuales y futuras y servicios.

French:

Lorsque vous envisagez vos contributions de don pour l'année prochaine, nous demandons que vous envisagez de soutenir votre communauté en soutenant le centre communautaire pour les enfants de Cordova. Le centre est un organisme sans but lucratif offrant des activités éducatives et récréatives pour les enfants. S'il vous plaît arrêter pour une visite. Notre personnel dévoué sera disponible pour discuter avec vous des services offerts par le centre, comment vos dollars de dons sont dépensés et fournir des informations sur les services et les activités actuelles et futures.

"Children are our most valuable natural resources." ~ Herbert Hoover

770 Sunrise Terrace ◆ Santa Fe, NM 87509 ◆ 505-555-7700

Case Study

Part

1

Data Files

You work in the executive offices at Nickell Industries and have been asked to develop a writing manual for employees. The company has not used a consistent theme when formatting documents, so you decide to choose a theme and use it when formatting all Nickell documents. Open **NIManual.docx** and then save the document and name it **2-NIManual**. Check the spelling and grammar in the document and then make the following changes to it:

- Insert a section break at the beginning of the title *Editing and Proofreading.*
- Apply styles of your choosing to the titles and headings in the document.
- Apply the theme you have chosen for company documents.
- Insert headers and/or footers.
- Create a cover page.
- Save the document.

Part

2

As you review the writing manual document you have created for Nickell Industries, you decide to highlight the points for developing sections of documents. You decide that a vertical block list SmartArt graphic will present the ideas in an easy-to-read format and provide some visual interest to the manual. Insert a page break at the end of **2-NIManual.docx**, type the title *Developing a Document*, and insert the following in the appropriate shapes:

Beginning

- Introduce main idea.
- Get reader's attention.
- Establish positive tone.

Middle

- Provide detail for main idea.
- Lead reader to intended conclusion.

End

- State conclusion.
- State action reader should take.

Apply colors that follow the theme you have chosen for company documents. Save the document.

Part

3

While working on the writing manual for Nickell Industries, you decide to purchase some reference books on grammar and punctuation. Using the Internet, search bookstores for books that provide information on grammar and punctuation and then choose three books. You know that the books will be purchased soon, so you decide to add the information in the writing manual document, telling readers what reference books are available. Include this information on a separate page at the end of **2-NIManual.docx**. Save, print, and then close the document.

Part

4

Nickell Industries does business in other countries, including Mexico. One of the executives in the Finance Department has asked you to translate into Spanish some terms that will be used to develop an invoice.

Create a document that translates the following terms from English to Spanish and also include in the document the steps for translating text. Your reason for doing this is that if the executive knows the steps, she can translate the text at her own computer.

- city
- telephone
- invoice
- product
- description
- total

Format the document with the theme you have chosen for company documents and add any other enhancements to improve the appearance of the document. Save the completed document and name it **2-NITranslations**. Print and then close **2-NITranslations.docx**.

Automating and Customizing Formatting

Study Tools

Study tools include a presentation and a list of chapter Quick Steps and Hint margin notes. Use these resources to help you further develop and review skills learned in this chapter.

Concepts Check

Check your understanding by identifying application tools used in this chapter. If you are a SNAP user, launch the Concepts Check from your Assignments page.

Recheck

Check your understanding by taking this quiz. If you are a SNAP user, launch the Recheck from your Assignments page.

Skills Exercise

Additional activities are available to SNAP users. If you are a SNAP user, access these activities from your Assignments page.

Skills Assessment

Assessment

✓ 1

Data Files

Format a Health Plan Document with AutoCorrect and Building Blocks

1. Open **KLHPlan.docx** and then save it with the name **3-KLHPlan**.
2. Add the following text to AutoCorrect:
   a. Insert *kl* in the *Replace* text box and insert *Key Life Health Plan* in the *With* text box.
   b. Insert *m* in the *Replace* text box and insert *medical* in the *With* text box.
3. With the insertion point positioned at the beginning of the document, type the text shown in Figure WB-3.1.
4. Make the following changes to the document:
   a. Apply the Heading 1 style to the title *Key Life Health Plan*.
   b. Apply the Heading 2 style to the four headings in the document.
   c. Apply the Lines (Simple) style set.
   d. Apply the Frame theme.
5. Insert the Ion (Dark) header building block.
6. Insert the Ion (Dark) footer building block. Click the *[DOCUMENT TITLE]* placeholder and then type key life health plan. Select the name at the right side of the footer and then type your first and last names.
7. Decrease the value in the *Footer from Bottom* measurement box to *0.3"*.
8. Double-click in the document.
9. Press Ctrl + End to move the insertion point to the end of the document, press the Enter key, and then insert the *FileName* field.
10. Press Shift + Enter and then insert the *PrintDate* field.

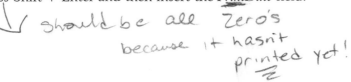

✓ should be all Zero's because it hasn't printed yet!

11. Save and then print **3-KLHPlan.docx**.
12. Delete the two entries you made at the AutoCorrect dialog box.
13. Close **3-KLHPlan.docx**.

Figure WB-3.1 Assessment 1

kl

How the Plan Works

When you enroll in the kl, you and each eligible family member select a plan option. A kl option includes a main m clinic, any affiliated satellite clinics, and designated hospitals. Family members may choose different m plan options and can easily change options.

Some m plan options do not require you to choose a primary care physician. This means a member may self-refer for specialty care within that m plan option. However, members are encouraged to establish an ongoing relationship with a primary care physician and develop a valuable partnership in the management of their m care.

kl provides coverage for emergency m services outside the service area. If the m emergency is not life threatening, call your primary care physician to arrange for care before going to an emergency facility. If you have a life-threatening emergency, go directly to the nearest appropriate facility. Any follow-up care to emergency m services must be coordinated within your plan option.

Assessment 2

Data Files

Format a Property Protection Issues Report

1. Open **ProtectIssues.docx** and then save it with the name **3-ProtectIssues**.
2. Make the following changes to the document:
   a. Select the entire document and then change the spacing after paragraphs to 6 points.
   b. Press Ctrl + Home and then press Ctrl + Enter to insert a hard page break.
   c. Apply the Heading 1 style to the two titles (*PROPERTY PROTECTION ISSUES* and *REFERENCES*).
   d. Apply the Heading 2 style to the three headings in the document.
   e. Apply the Banded theme.
   f. Apply the Paper theme colors.
   g. Format the paragraphs of text below the title *REFERENCES* using a hanging indent.
   h. Indent the second paragraph in the *Fair Use* section 0.5 inch from the left and right margins.
3. Press Ctrl + Home to move the insertion point to the beginning of the document and then insert the Automatic Table 2 table of contents building block.
4. Make sure the Heading 1 style is applied to the title *Table of Contents*.
5. Insert the Banded header building block, click the *[DOCUMENT TITLE]* placeholder, and then type property protection issues.
6. Insert the Banded footer building block.
7. Double-click in the document.

8. Press Ctrl + Home and then insert the Banded cover page building block with the following specifications:
   a. Select the title *PROPERTY PROTECTION ISSUES* and then change the font size to 28 points.
   b. Select the name near the bottom of the cover page above the company name placeholder and then type your first and last names.
   c. Click the *[COMPANY NAME]* placeholder and then type woodland legal services.
   d. Select and then delete the company address placeholder.
9. Press Ctrl + End to move the insertion point to the end of the document, press the Enter key, and then insert a field that will insert the file name.
10. Press Shift + Enter and then insert a field that will insert the current date and time.
11. Save, print, and then close **3-ProtectIssues.docx**.

Assessment

3

Data Files ▶

Create Building Blocks and Prepare an Agreement

1. Press Ctrl + N to open a blank document and then save the blank document as a template in your WL2C3 folder and name it **3-WLTemplate**. (Make sure you change the *Save as type* option at the Save As dialog box to *Word Template (*.dotx)*.)
2. Close **3-WLTemplate.dotx**.
3. Use File Explorer to open a document based on **3-WLTemplate.dotx** located in your WL2C3 folder.
4. Insert **WLFooter.docx** into the document. *Hint: Use the Object button arrow on the Insert tab.*
5. Select the line of text containing the address and telephone number (including the paragraph mark that ends the line). Save the selected text in a custom building block in the Footer gallery, name the building block *WLFooter* and save it in **3-WLTemplate.docx**. *Hint: Use the Footer button to save the content to the Footer gallery.*
6. Select the entire document, press the Delete key, and then insert **WLHeading.docx** into the current document. *Hint: Use the Object button arrow on the Insert tab.*
7. Select the two lines of text (including the paragraph mark at the end of the second line), save the selected text in a custom building block in the Quick Part gallery, name the building block *WLHeading* and save it in **3-WLTemplate.docx**.
8. Select the entire document, press the Delete key, and then type the text shown in Figure WB-3.2. (Make sure you apply bold formatting to *Fees*).
9. Select the entire document, save the selected text in a custom building block in the AutoText gallery, name the building block *WLFeesPara* and save it in **3-WLTemplate.docx**.
10. Close the document without saving it and, at the message that displays asking if you want to save changes to the template, click the Save button.
11. Use File Explorer to open a blank document based on **3-WLTemplate.dotx**.
12. At the blank document, create an agreement with the following specifications:
    a. Insert the WLHeading custom building block in the Quick Part gallery.
    b. Press the Enter key and then insert the WLFeesPara custom building block in the AutoText gallery.
    c. Insert **WLRepAgrmnt.docx**. *Hint: Use the Object button arrow on the Insert tab.*
    d. Insert the WLFooter custom building block. *Hint: Do this with the Footer button.*

13. Click the Close Header and Footer button and then save the completed agreement and name it **3-WLRepAgrmnt**.
14. Print and then close **3-WLRepAgrmnt.docx**.
15. Use File Explorer to open a document based on **3-WLTemplate.dotx**.
16. Click the Insert tab, click the Quick Parts button, and then point to *AutoText*.

Stop → here 17. Press the Print Screen button on your keyboard and then click in the document.
18. At the blank document, click the Paste button.
19. Print the document and then close it without saving it.

Submit Screen shot!

Figure WB-3.2 Assessment 3

> **Fees:** My hourly rate is $350, billed in one-sixth (1/6th) of an hour increments. All time spent on work performed, including meetings, telephone calls, correspondences, and emails, will be billed at the hourly rate set forth in this paragraph. Additional expenses such as out-of-pocket expenses for postage, courier fees, photocopying charges, long distance telephone charges, and search fees, will be charged at the hourly rate set forth in this paragraph.

Assessment 4

Create a Custom Tab and Group

1. At a blank screen, create a new tab with the following specifications:
    a. Insert the new tab after the *View* tab option in the list box at the Word Options dialog box with *Customize Ribbon* selected.
    b. Rename the tab *C3* followed by your initials.
    c. Rename the custom group below your new tab as *File Management*.
    d. Change the *Choose commands from* option to *File Tab*.
    e. From the list box at the left side of the dialog box, add the following commands to the File Management group on the new tab: Close File, Open, Quick Print, and Save As Other Format.
    f. Change the *Choose commands from* option to *Popular Commands*.
    g. From the list box at the left side of the dialog box, add the New File command.
    h. Click OK to close the Word Options dialog box.
2. At the blank screen, click your new tab (the one that begins with *C3* and is followed by your initials).
3. Click the Open button in the File Management group on your new tab.
4. At the Open backstage area, click **3-WLRepAgrmnt.docx** at the beginning of the *Recent* option list.
5. Use the Save As button in the File Management group on the new tab to save the document and name it **3-RepAgrmnt**.
6. Save the document in the Word 97-2003 format by completing the following steps:
    a. Make sure the new tab is active.
    b. Click the Save As button arrow.
    c. Click *Word 97-2003 Document* at the drop-down list.
    d. At the Save As dialog box with *Word 97-2003 Document (*.doc)* selected in the *Save as type* option box, type 3-WLRA-Word97-2003Format and then press the Enter key.
    e. Close the document by clicking the Close button in the File Management group on the new tab.

7. Click the Open button on the new tab and then click *3-RepAgrmnt.docx* in the *Recent* option list.
8. Send the document to the printer by clicking the Quick Print button on the new tab.
9. Close the document by clicking the Close button on the new tab.
10. Click the New Blank Document button on the new tab.
11. At the blank document, click the New Blank Document button on the new tab. (You now have two blank documents open.)
12. Click the Insert tab, click the Screenshot button, and then click *Screen Clipping* at the drop-down list.
13. When the first blank document displays in a dimmed manner, use the mouse to select the Quick Access Toolbar and ribbon (including the new tab with the File Management group buttons you created).
14. Print the document containing the screen clipping and then close the document without saving it.
15. Display the Word Options dialog box with *Customize Ribbon* selected and then reset the ribbon back to the default.

Assessment
5

Insert an Equation Building Block

1. The Building Blocks Organizer dialog box contains a number of predesigned equations that you can insert in a document. At a blank document, display the Building Blocks Organizer dialog box and then insert one of the predesigned equations.
2. Select the equation and then click the Equation Tools Design tab. Notice the groups of commands available for editing an equation.
3. Type the steps you followed to insert the equation and then type a list of the groups available on the Equation Tools Design tab.
4. Save the document and name it **3-Equation**. Print and then close the document.

Visual Benchmark

Create an Agreement with Building Blocks and AutoCorrect Text

1. Use File Explorer to open a document based on **3-WLTemplate.dotx**.
2. Create the document shown in Figure WB-3.3 with the following specifications:
   a. Create AutoCorrect entries for *Woodland Legal Services* (use *wls*) and *Till-Harris Management* (use *thm*). Press the Enter key twice and then type the text in Figure WB-3.3 using the AutoCorrect entries you created.
   b. Insert the WLHeading building block at the beginning of the document and insert the WLFooter as a footer.
   c. Justify the six paragraphs of text in the document and then center-align the signature lines.
3. Save the completed document and name it **3-THMAgrmnt**.
4. Print and then close **3-THMAgrmnt.docx**.
5. Open a blank document, display the AutoCorrect dialog box, and then display the *thm* entry. Press Alt + Print Screen, close the dialog box, close the Word Options dialog box, and then click the Paste button at the blank document. (This inserts an image of the AutoCorrect dialog box. Alt + Print Screen makes a capture of the active dialog box.)
6. Press Ctrl + End and then press the Enter key.

7. Complete steps similar to those in Step 5 to make a screen capture of the AutoCorrect dialog box with the *wls* entry displayed and insert the screen capture image in the document (below the first screen capture image).
8. Decrease the sizes of both images so they display on one page. Print and then close the document without saving it.
9. At a blank document, delete the *wls* and *thm* AutoCorrect entries.

Submit Screenshots

Figure WB-3.3 Visual Benchmark

REPRESENTATION AGREEMENT

Carlos Sawyer, Attorney at Law

This agreement is made between Carlos Sawyer of Woodland Legal Services and Till-Harris Management for legal services to be provided by Woodland Legal Services.

Legal Representation: Woodland Legal Services will perform the legal services required by Till-Harris Management, keep Till-Harris Management informed of progress and developments, and respond promptly to Till-Harris Management's inquiries and communications.

Attorney's Fees and Costs: Till-Harris Management will pay Woodland Legal Services for attorney's fees for legal services provided under this agreement at the hourly rate of the individuals providing the services. Under this agreement, Till-Harris Management will pay all costs incurred by Woodland Legal Services for representation of Till-Harris Management. Costs will be advanced by Woodland Legal Services and then billed to Till-Harris Management unless the costs can be met from deposits.

Deposit for Fees: Till-Harris Management will pay to Woodland Legal Services an initial deposit of $5,000, to be received by Woodland Legal Services on or before November 1, 2018. Twenty percent of the deposit is nonrefundable and will be applied against attorney's fees. The refundable portion will be deposited by Woodland Legal Services in an interest-bearing trust account. Till-Harris Management authorizes Woodland Legal Services to withdraw the principal from the trust account to pay attorney's fees in excess of the nonrefundable portion.

Statement and Payments: Woodland Legal Services will send Till-Harris Management monthly statements indicating attorney's fees and costs incurred, amounts applied from deposits, and current balance owed. If no attorney's fees or costs are incurred for a particular month, the statement may be held and combined with that for the following month. Any balance will be paid in full within 30 days after the statement is mailed.

Effective Date of Agreement: The effective date of this agreement will be the date when it is executed by both parties.

Client: _____ Date: _____

Attorney: _____ Date: _____

7110 FIFTH STREET ◆ SUITE 200 ◆ OMAHA NE 68207 ◆ 402-555-7110

Case Study

You have been hired as the office manager for Highland Construction Company. The address of the company is 9025 Palmer Park Boulevard, Colorado Springs, CO 80904 and the telephone number is (719) 555-4575. You are responsible for designing business documents that have a consistent visual style and formatting. You decide that your first task is to create a letterhead document. Press Ctrl + N to open a blank document and then save the document as a template named *HCCTemplate* in your WL2C3 folder. Close the template document. Use File Explorer to open a blank document based on **HCCTemplate.dotx**. At the blank document based on the template, create a letterhead that includes the company name, address, and telephone number, along with an image and/or any other elements to add visual interest. Select the letterhead text and element(s) and then create a building block in the Quick Part gallery named *HCCLtrhd* that is saved in **HCCTemplate.dotx**. Create the following additional building block for your company. (You decide on the names and save the building blocks in **HCCTemplate.dotx**.)

- Create a building block footer that contains a border line (in a color matching the colors in the letterhead) and the company slogan:
    Building Dreams Since 1985
- Create the following complimentary close building block:
    Sincerely,

    Your Name
    Office Manager
- Create the following company name and address building block:
    Mr. Eric Rashad
    Roswell Industries
    1020 Wasatch Street
    Colorado Springs, CO 80902
- Create the following company name and address building block:
    Ms. Claudia Sanborn
    S & S Supplies
    537 Constitution Avenue
    Colorado Springs, CO 80911

Select and then delete the contents of the document. Close the document without saving it. At the message that displays asking if you want to save changes to the template, click the Save button.

Data Files

Use File Explorer to open a document based on **HCCTemplate.dotx**. Apply the No Spacing style and then create a letter to Eric Rashad by inserting the Highland Construction Company letterhead (the HCCLtrhd building block). Press the Enter key, type today's date, press the Enter key four times, and then insert the Eric Rashad building block. Press the Enter key, type an appropriate salutation (such as *Dear Mr. Rashad:*), insert the file named **HCCLetter.docx**, and then insert your complimentary close building block. Finally, insert the footer building block you created for the company. Check the letter and modify the spacing as needed. Save the letter and name it **3-RashadLtr**. Print and then close the letter. Complete similar steps to create a letter to Claudia Sanborn. Save the completed letter and name it **3-SanbornLtr**. Print and then close the letter.

Part 3

Use File Explorer to open a document based on **HCCTemplate.dotx**. Insert the Highland Construction Company letterhead building block you created in Part 1, type the title *Company Services*, and then insert a SmartArt graphic of your choosing that contains the following text:

Residential Construction
Commercial Construction
Design Consultation
Site Preparation

Apply a heading style to the *Company Services* title, insert the company footer building block, and then save the document and name it **3-CoServices**. Print and then close the document.

Part 4

Data Files

Create an AutoCorrect entry that will replace *hcc* with *Highland Construction Company* and *bca* with *Building Construction Agreement*. Use File Explorer to open a document based on **HCCTemplate.dotx**. Insert **HCCAgrmnt.docx** and then type the text shown in Figure WB-3.4 at the beginning of the document. Apply or insert the following in the document:

- Insert at the end of the document a date printed field and a file name field.
- Insert your footer building block as a footer.
- Insert a cover page of your choosing.

Add or apply any other enhancements to improve the appearance of the document and then save the document and name it **3-HCCAgrmnt**. Print and then close the document.

Part 5

Make sure you are connected to the Internet and then display the New backstage area. Choose a business card template, download it, and then create business cards for Highland Construction Company. Include your name and title (Office Manager) on the cards. Save the completed business cards document and name it **3-HCCBusCards**. Print and then close the document. Delete the AutoCorrect entries *hcc* and *bca*.

Figure WB-3.4 Case Study, Part 4

---

bca

THIS bca made this _____day of _____, 2018 by and between hcc and _____, hereinafter referred to as "owner," for the considerations hereinafter named, hcc and owner agree as follows:

Financing Arrangements: The owner will obtain a construction loan to finance construction under this bca. If adequate financing has not been arranged within 30 days of the date of this bca, or the owner cannot provide evidence to hcc of other financial ability to pay the full amount, then hcc may treat this bca as null and void, and retain the down payment made on the execution of this bca.

> **Study Tools**

Study tools include a presentation and a list of chapter Quick Steps and Hint margin notes. Use these resources to help you further develop and review skills learned in this chapter.

> **Concepts Check**

Check your understanding by identifying application tools used in this chapter. If you are a SNAP user, launch the Concepts Check from your Assignments page.

> **Recheck**

Check your understanding by taking this quiz. If you are a SNAP user, launch the Recheck from your Assignments page.

Skills Exercise

Additional activities are available to SNAP users. If you are a SNAP user, access these activities from your Assignments page.

Skills Assessment

Assessment

X **1**

> Data Files

Create and Apply Custom Themes to a Medical Plans Document

1. At a blank document, create custom theme colors named with your initials that make the following color changes:
   a. Change the Accent 1 color to standard dark red (first option in the *Standard Colors* section).   p.125
   b. Change the Accent 5 color to Gold, Accent 4, Darker 50% (eighth column, bottom row in the *Theme Colors* section).
2. Create custom theme fonts named with your initials that change the heading font to Corbel and the body font to Garamond.
3. Click the Theme Effects button and then click *Top Shadow* at the drop-down gallery (first column, third row).
4. Save the custom document theme and name it with your initials. ***Hint: Do this with the Save Current Theme option at the Themes button drop-down gallery.***
5. Close the document without saving the changes.
6. Open **KLHPlan.docx** and then save it with the name **4-KLHPlan**.
7. Make the following changes to the document:
   a. Apply the Lines (Simple) style set.
   b. With the insertion point at the beginning of the document, type the title Key Life Health Plan.
   c. Apply the Heading 1 style to the title.
   d. Apply the Heading 2 style to the three headings in the document.
8. Move the insertion point to the end of the document, press Ctrl + Enter to insert a page break, and then insert the document **KLHPlanGraphic.docx**. ***Hint: Do this with the Object button arrow on the Insert tab.***

9. Apply the custom document theme you created by clicking the Design tab, clicking the Themes button, and then clicking the custom document theme named with your initials.
10. Save, print, and then close **4-KLHPlan.docx**.
11. At a blank document, delete the custom theme colors named with your initials, the custom theme fonts named with your initials, and the custom document theme named with your initials.

Assessment

2

Data Files

Record and Run Formatting Macros

1. Open **MacroText.docx** and then create a macro named *XXXTitle* (where *XXX* is your initials) with the following specifications:
   a. Position the insertion point at the beginning of the word *Title* and then turn on the macro recorder.
   b. Press the F8 function key and then press the End key.
   c. Click the Center button and then click the Bold button.
   d. Click the *Font Size* option box arrow and then click *14* at the drop-down gallery.
   e. Click the Shading button arrow and then click *Blue, Accent 1, Lighter 40%* (fifth column, fourth row in the *Theme Colors* section).
   f. Click the Borders button arrow and then click the *Bottom Border* option.
   g. Turn off the macro recorder.
2. Create a macro named *XXXHd* (where *XXX* is your initials) with the following specifications:
   a. Position the insertion point at the beginning of the word *Heading* and then turn on the macro recorder.
   b. Press the F8 function key and then press the End key.
   c. Click the Bold button and then click the Italic button.
   d. Click the *Font Size* option box arrow and then click *12* at the drop-down gallery.
   e. Click the Shading button arrow and then click *Blue, Accent 1, Lighter 80%* (fifth column, second row in the *Theme Colors* section).
   f. Turn off the macro recorder.
3. Create a macro named *XXXDocFont* (where *XXX* is your initials) that selects the entire document and then changes the font to Cambria. Assign the macro the keyboard shortcut Alt + D.
4. Close **MacroText.docx** without saving it.
5. Open **WebReport.docx** and then save it with the name **4-WebReport**.
6. Press Alt + D to run the XXXDocFont macro.
7. Run the XXXTitle macro for the two titles in the document: *Navigating the Web* and *Searching the Web*.
8. Run the XXXHd macro for the four headings in the document: *IPs and URLs*, *Browsing Web Pages*, *Search Engines*, and *How Search Engines Work*.
9. Save, print, and then close **4-WebReport.docx**.
10. Delete the macros you created in this assessment: XXXDocFont, XXXTitle, and XXXHd.

Assessment

3

Data Files

Format and Navigate in a Corporate Report Document

1. Open **DIReport.docx** and then save it with the name **4-DIReport**.
2. Move the insertion point to any character in the second paragraph (the paragraph that begins *Assist the company's board of directors in fulfilling*), turn on the display of the Styles task pane, apply the Intense Quote style to the paragraph, and then turn off the display of the Styles task pane.

3. Apply the Lines (Distinctive) style set.
4. Turn on the display of bookmarks.
5. Move the insertion point to the end of the third paragraph (the paragraph that begins *The audit committee selects*) and then insert a bookmark named *Audit*.
6. Move the insertion point to the end of the first paragraph in the section FEES TO INDEPENDENT AUDITOR, following the *(Excel worksheet)* text, and then insert a bookmark named *Audit_Fees*.
7. Move the insertion point to the end of the last paragraph and then insert a bookmark named *Compensation*.
8. Navigate in the document using the bookmarks.
9. Move the insertion point to the end of the first paragraph in the section COMMITTEE RESPONSIBILITIES, press the spacebar, and then insert a hyperlink to the Audit_Fees bookmark.
10. Select the text *(Excel worksheet)* at the end of the first paragraph in the section FEES TO INDEPENDENT AUDITOR and then insert a hyperlink to the Excel file **AuditorFees.xlsx**.
11. Move the insertion point to the end of the document, click the image, and then insert a hyperlink to the Word document **DIGraphic.docx**. At the Insert Hyperlink dialog box, create a ScreenTip with the text *Click to view a long-term incentives graphic*.
12. Press and hold down the Ctrl key, click the *(Excel worksheet)* hyperlink, and then release the Ctrl key. Print the Excel worksheet that displays by clicking the File tab, clicking the *Print* option, and then clicking the Print button in the Print backstage area.
13. Close the Excel program without saving the file.
14. Press and hold down the Ctrl key, click the image to display the Word document containing the graphic, and then release the Ctrl key. Print and then close the graphic document.
15. Save, print, and then close **4-DIReport.docx**.

Assessment 4

Data Files

Assign Macros to the Quick Access Toolbar

1. In this chapter, you learned how to record a macro and assign it to a keyboard command. A macro can also be assigned to a button on the Quick Access Toolbar. Using the Help feature, search for and then read the article "Create or run a macro." Learn how to assign a macro to a button.
2. Open **NSSMacroText.docx** and then use the document to create the following macros:
   a. Create a macro named *XXXNSSDocFormat* (where *XXX* is your initials) and assign it to a button on the Quick Access Toolbar. (You determine the button icon.) The macro should select the entire document (use Ctrl + A), apply the No Spacing style (click the *No Spacing* style in the Styles group), change the line spacing to double (press Ctrl + 2), and change the font to Constantia.
   b. Create a macro named *XXXNSSHeading* (where *XXX* is your initials) and assign it to a button on the Quick Access Toolbar. (You determine the button icon.) The macro should select a line of text (at the beginning of the line, press the F8 function key and then press the End key), change the font size to 12 points, apply bold formatting, center the text, and then deselect the text.
3. Close **NSSMacroText.docx** without saving the changes.
4. Open **EmpComp.docx** and then save it with the name **4-EmpComp**.
5. Click the button on the Quick Access Toolbar to run the XXXNSSDocFormat macro.

6. Run the XXXNSSHeading macro (using the button on the Quick Access Toolbar) for the title *COMPENSATION* and the five headings in the document.
7. Keep the heading *Overtime* with the paragraph of text that follows it.
8. Save, print, and then close **4-EmpComp.docx**.
9. Open a blank document and then open another blank document. Make a screenshot of the Quick Access Toolbar. (Use the *Screen Clippings* option from the Screenshot button drop-down list.) Print the document containing the screenshot and then close the document without saving it.
10. At the remaining blank document, delete the macro buttons from the Quick Access Toolbar and then delete the macros from the Macros dialog box.
11. Remove the Developer tab from the ribbon. (Do this by displaying the Word Options dialog box with *Customize Ribbon* selected in the left panel. Remove the check mark from the *Developer* check box and then click OK to close the dialog box.)

Visual Benchmark

Insert Smartart Graphics in a Business Document

1. Open **DIRevenues.docx** and then save it with the name **4-DIRevenues**.
2. Create the following custom theme colors (named with your first and last names) with the following changes:
   a. Change the Text/Background - Dark 2 color to Orange, Accent 2, Darker 50% (sixth column, last row in the *Theme Colors* section).
   b. Change the Accent 1 color to Green, Accent 6, Darker 50% (tenth column, last row in the *Theme Colors* section).
   c. Change the Accent 4 color to Orange, Accent 2, Darker 50%.
   d. Change the Accent 6 color to Green, Accent 6, Darker 25% (tenth column, fifth row in the *Theme Colors* section).
3. Create the following custom theme fonts (named with your first and last names) with the following changes:
   a. Change the heading font to Copperplate Gothic Bold.
   b. Change the body font to Constantia.
4. Apply the Riblet theme effect.
5. Save the custom document theme and name it *WL2C4* followed by your initials. *Hint: Do this with the* **Save Current Theme** *option at the Themes button drop-down gallery.*
6. Center the title and reposition the SmartArt graphic as shown in Figure WB-4.1.
7. Save, print, and then close **4-DIRevenues.docx**.
8. Open **DICorporate.docx** and then save it with the name **4-DICorporate**.
9. Apply the WL2C4 (followed by your initials) custom document theme to the document.
10. Center the title and reposition the SmartArt graphic as shown in Figure WB-4.2.
11. Save, print, and then close **4-DICorporate.docx**.
12. At a blank document, use the Print Screen button to make a screen capture of the Theme Colors drop-down gallery (make sure your custom theme colors display), a screen capture of the Theme Fonts drop-down gallery (make sure your custom theme fonts display), and a screen capture of the Save Current Theme dialog box (make sure your custom document themes display). Insert all three screen capture images on the same page. (You will need to size the images.)

28   Word Level 2 | Unit 1   Chapter 4 | Customizing Themes, Creating Macros, and Navigating in a Document

Figure WB-4.1 Visual Benchmark

DEARBORN INDUSTRIES

REVENUES

We are evaluating markets for our current and future products. Prior to the fourth quarter of 2018, we recorded revenues as a result of development contracts with government entities focused on the design of flywheel technologies. We have produced and placed several development prototypes with potential customers and shipped preproduction units.

RESEARCH AND DEVELOPMENT

Our cost of research and development consists primarily of the cost of compensation and benefits for research and support staff, as well as materials and supplies used in the engineering design and development process. These costs decreased significantly during 2018 as we focused on reducing our expenditure rate by reducing product design and development activities.

PREFERRED STOCK DIVIDENDS

Prior to our initial public offering of our common stock, we had various classes of preferred stock outstanding, each of which was entitled to receive dividends. We accrued dividend expenses monthly according to the requirements of each class of preferred stock.

DEARBORN INDUSTRIES

CORPORATE VISION

Dearborn Industries will be the leading developer of clean and environmentally friendly products. Building on strong leadership, development, and resources, we will provide superior-quality products and services to our customers and consumers around the world.

CORPORATE VALUES

We value the environment in which we live, and we will work to produce and maintain energy-efficient and environmentally safe products and strive to reduce our carbon footprint on the environment.

CORPORATE LEADERSHIP

Dearborn Industries employees conduct business under the leadership of the chief executive officer, who is subject to the oversight and direction of the board of directors. Four vice presidents work with the chief executive officer to manage and direct business.

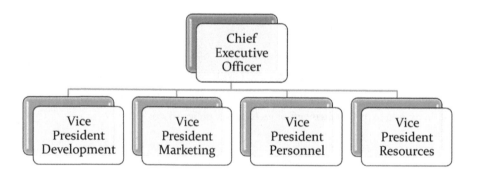

13. Save the document and name it **4-ScreenImages**.
14. Print and then close **4-ScreenImages.docx**.
15. At a blank document, delete the custom color theme you created, as well as the custom font theme and the custom document theme.

Case Study

You work for Jackson Photography and have been asked by the owner to create a new letterhead for the company. Open **JPLtrd.docx**, save the document as a template and name it **JPTemplate** in your WL2C4 folder, and then customize the text and image to create an attractive and professional-looking letterhead. Create a building block with the letterhead that is saved in **JPTemplate.dotx**. Delete the letterhead text and element(s) and then save and close the template.

At a blank document, create and then save custom theme colors that match the letterhead you created for Jackson Photography in Part 1. Create and then save custom theme fonts that apply the Arial font to the headings and the Constantia font to the body text. Apply a custom theme effect of your choosing. Save the custom document theme in the Save Current Theme dialog box and name it with your initials followed by *JP*.

Use File Explorer to open a blank document based on **JPTemplate.dotx**. Insert the Jackson Photography letterhead building block you created in Part 1, type the title Photography Services, and then insert a SmartArt graphic of your choosing that contains the following text:

- Wedding Photography
- Sports Portraits
- Senior Portraits
- Family Portraits
- Processing

Apply a heading style to the title *Photography Services*, apply the custom document theme to the document, and then save the document and name it **4-JPServices**. Print and then close **4-JPServices.docx**.

Open **JPReport.docx** and then save it with the name **4-JPReport**. Format the report by applying or inserting the following in the document:

- Apply your custom document theme.
- Apply the Intense Quote style to the quote at the beginning and the quote at the end of the document.
- Insert a footer of your choosing.

Apply any other enhancements to improve the appearance of the document. Save **4-JPReport.docx**.

With **4-JPReport.docx** open, insert at the end of the third paragraph in the section *Photography* a hyperlink that links to **KodakHistory.docx**. Using the Internet, research and locate at least one company that sells digital cameras. At the end of the document, insert text that tells the reader to click the hyperlink to link to that particular website and then insert the hyperlink to the site you found. Save, print, and then close **4-JPReport.docx**.

Unit 1 Performance Assessment

> **Data Files**
>
> Before beginning chapter work, copy the WL2U1 folder to
> your storage medium and then make WL2U1 the active folder.

Assessing Proficiency

In this unit, you have learned how to customize the spelling, grammar, and
AutoCorrect features in a document; format documents with special features, such
as customized bulleted and numbered lists, headers, footers, and page numbering;
automate formatting with macros; and apply and customize building blocks,
themes, style sets, and styles.

Assessment

1

Data Files

Format a Stock Awards Document

1. Open **CMStocks.docx** and then save it with the name **U1-CMStocks**.
2. Apply the Title style to the title *Clearline Manufacturing*.
3. Apply the Heading 1 style to the headings *Stock Awards* and *Employee Stock Plan*.
4. Apply the Centered style set.
5. Select the bulleted paragraphs of text and then define a new picture bullet using **BlueCircle.png**.
6. Select the lines of text below the heading *Employee Stock Plan* and then apply a multilevel list (middle option in top row of the *List Library* section of the Multilevel List button drop-down gallery).
7. With the text still selected, define a new multilevel list that inserts capital letters followed by periods (A., B., C.) for level 2 and arabic numbers followed by periods (1., 2., 3.) for level 3. (Make sure the new multilevel list applies to the selected text.)
8. Save, print, and then close **U1-CMStocks.docx**.

Assessment

2

Data Files

Format a Future of Computer Ethics Report

1. Open **CompEthics.docx** and then save it with the name **U1-CompEthics**.
2. Keep the heading *Self-Replicating Robots* (at the bottom of the first page) together with the paragraph of text that follows it.
3. Keep the title *REFERENCES* (at the bottom of the second page) together with the paragraph of text that follows it.

33

4. Insert the *FileName* and *PrintDate* fields at the end of the document (on separate lines).
5. Create an odd page footer that prints the document title, *Computer Ethics*, at the left margin and the page number at the right margin. Also create an even page footer that prints the page number at the left margin and the document title at the right margin.
6. Save, print, and then close **U1-CompEthics.docx**.

Assessment

3

Create and Format a Column Chart

1. At a blank document, use the data in Figure WB-U1.1 to create a column chart with the following specifications:
   a. Choose the 3-D Clustered Column chart type.
   b. Apply the Layout 3 chart layout.
   c. Apply the Style 5 chart style.
   d. Change the chart title to *2018 Sales*.
   e. Insert a data table with legend keys. **Hint: Do this with the Chart Elements button outside the upper right corner of the selected chart.**
   f. Select the chart area, apply the Subtle Effect - Green, Accent 6 shape style (last column, fourth row in the *Theme Styles* section), and apply the Offset Bottom shadow shape effect (second column, first row in the *Outer* section).
   g. Select the series *Second Half* and then apply the standard dark red shape fill (first option in the *Standard Colors* section).
   h. Change the chart height to 4 inches and the chart width to 6.25 inches.
   i. Use the Position button in the Arrange group to position the chart in the middle center of the page with square text wrapping.
2. Save the document with the name **U1-SalesChart**.
3. Print **U1-SalesChart.docx**.
4. With the chart selected, display the Excel worksheet and edit the data in the worksheet by changing the following:
   a. Change the amount in cell C2 from *$285,450* to *$302,500*.
   b. Change the amount in cell C4 from *$180,210* to *$190,150*.
5. Save, print, and then close **U1-SalesChart.docx**.

Figure WB-U1.1 Assessment 3

Salesperson	First Half	Second Half
Bratton	$235,500	$285,450
Daniels	$300,570	$250,700
Hughes	$170,200	$180,210
Marez	$308,520	$346,400

Assessment

4

Create and Format a Pie Chart

1. At a blank document, use the data in Figure WB-U1.2 to create a pie chart with the following specifications:
   a. Apply the Layout 6 chart layout.
   b. Apply the Style 3 chart style.
   c. Change the chart title to *District Expenditures*.

    d. Move the legend to the left side of the chart.

    e. Select the chart area, apply the Gold, Accent 4, Lighter 80% shape fill (eighth column, second row in the *Theme Colors* section), and apply the Gray-50%, 11 pt glow, Accent color 3 glow shape effect (third column, third row in the *Glow Variations* section).

    f. Select the legend and apply a Blue shape outline (eighth option in the *Standard Colors* section).

    g. Apply the WordArt style Fill - Blue, Accent 5, Outline - Background 1, Hard Shadow - Accent 5 (third column, third row) to the chart title text.

    h. Move the data labels to the inside ends of the pie pieces.

    i. Select the legend and center it between the left edge of the chart border and the pie.

    j. Use the Position button in the Arrange group to center the chart at the top of the page with square text wrapping.

2. Save the document with the name **U1-ExpendChart**.
3. Print and then close **U1-ExpendChart.docx**.

Figure WB-U1.2 Assessment 4

	Percentage
Basic Education	42%
Special Needs	20%
Support Services	19%
Vocational	11%
Compensatory	8%

Assessment 5

Data Files

Navigate in a Smoke Detector Report

1. Open **SmokeDetectors.docx** and then save it with the name **U1-SmokeDetectors**.
2. If necessary, turn on the display of bookmarks. (Do this at the Word Options dialog box with *Advanced* selected in the left panel.)
3. Move the insertion point to the end of the paragraph in the section *Types of Smoke Detectors* and then insert a bookmark named *Types*.
4. Move the insertion point to the end of the last paragraph in the section *Safety Tips* and then insert a bookmark named *Resources*.
5. Move the insertion point to the end of the first paragraph in the section *Taking Care of Smoke Detectors* (at the bottom of the second page) and then insert a bookmark named *Maintenance*.
6. Navigate in the document using the bookmarks.
7. Select the text *(NFPA website)* at the end of the first paragraph and then insert a hyperlink to the website www.nfpa.org.
8. Press and hold down the Ctrl key and then click the *(NFPA website)* hyperlink. At the NFPA home page, navigate to web pages that interest you and then close your browser.
9. Move the insertion point to the end of the document and then create a hyperlink with the image to the Word document **SmokeDetectorFacts.docx**.
10. Click outside the image to deselect it.

11. Press and hold down the Ctrl key and then click the image. At **SmokeDetectorFacts.docx**, read the information, print the document, and then close the document.
12. Save, print, and then close **U1-SmokeDetectors.docx**.

Assessment 6

Data Files

Format a Computer Devices Report

1. Open **CompDevices.docx** and then save it with the name **U1-CompDevices**.
2. With the insertion point at the beginning of the document, press Ctrl + Enter to insert a page break.
3. Apply the Heading 1 style to the two titles in the document: *COMPUTER INPUT DEVICES* and *COMPUTER OUTPUT DEVICES*.
4. Apply the Heading 2 style to the six headings in the document.
5. Apply the Minimalist style set.
6. Apply the Yellow Orange theme colors.
7. Apply the Corbel theme fonts.
8. Insert a section break that begins a new page at the beginning of the title *COMPUTER OUTPUT DEVICES* (located on the third page).
9. Create a footer for the first section in the document that prints *Computer Input Devices* at the left margin, the page number in the middle, and your first and last names at the right margin.
10. Edit the footer for the second section so it prints *Computer Output Devices* instead of *Computer Input Devices*. (Make sure you deactivate the *Link to Previous* feature.)
11. Move the insertion point to the beginning of the document and then insert the Slice (Dark) cover page. Type COMPUTER DEVICES as the document title and type Computer Input and Output Devices as the document subtitle.
12. Move the insertion point to the beginning of the second page (blank page) and then insert the Automatic Table 1 table of contents building block.
13. Save, print, and then close **U1-CompDevices.docx**.

Assessment 7

Data Files

Format a Building a Website Document

1. Open **BuildWebsite.docx** and then save it with the name **U1-BuildWebsite**.
2. Display the Word Options dialog box with *Proofing* selected in the left panel, remove the check mark from the *Ignore words in UPPERCASE* option, insert a check mark in the *Show readability statistics* check box, and then close the dialog box.
3. Complete a spelling and grammar check on the document and then proofread the document. Make any necessary changes not selected during the spelling and grammar check.
4. Format the document with the following:
   a. Apply the Title style to the title *Building a Website*; apply the Heading 1 style to the headings *Planning a Website*, *Choosing a Host*, and *Organizing the Site*; and apply the Heading 2 style to the subheadings *Free Web-Hosting Services*, *Free Hosting from ISPs*, and *Fee-Based Hosting Services*.
   b. Format the text (except the title) into two evenly spaced columns. Balance the end of the text on the second page.
   c. Apply the Shaded style set and then center the title.
   d. Apply the Blue Warm theme colors and the Garamond theme fonts.

    e. Insert the Ion (Dark) header building block.

    f. Insert the Ion (Dark) footer building block. Type BUILDING A WEBSITE as the document title and type your first and last names at the right side of the footer.

5. Display the Word Options dialog box with *Proofing* selected in the left panel, insert a check mark in the *Ignore words in UPPERCASE* check box, remove the check mark from the *Show readability statistics* check box, and then close the dialog box.

6. Save, print, and then close **U1-BuildWebsite.docx**.

Assessment

8

Format an Equipment Rental Agreement

1. At a blank document, create custom theme colors named with your initials that make the following color changes:

    a. Change the Text/Background - Dark 2 color to Orange, Accent 2, Darker 50% (sixth column, last row in the *Theme Colors* section).

    b. Change the Accent 1 color to Green, Accent 6, Darker 25% (tenth column, fifth row in the *Theme Colors* section).

2. Create custom theme fonts named with your initials that apply the Verdana font to the headings and the Cambria font to the body text.

3. Save the custom document theme and name it with your initials. (Do this with the *Save Current Theme* option at the Themes button drop-down gallery.)

4. Close the document without saving the changes.

5. Open **MRCForm.docx** and then save it with the name **U1-MRCForm**.

6. Search for all the occurrences of *mrc* and replace them with *Meridian Rental Company*.

7. Add the following text to AutoCorrect:

    a. Type mrc in the *Replace* text box and type Meridian Rental Company in the *With* text box.

    b. Type erag in the *Replace* text box and type Equipment Rental Agreement in the *With* text box.

8. Move the insertion point to the blank line below the heading *Default* (on the third page) and then type the text shown in Figure WB-U1.3. Use the Numbering feature to number each paragraph with a lowercase letter followed by a right parenthesis. (If the AutoCorrect feature capitalizes the first word after the letter and right parenthesis, use the AutoCorrect options button to return the letter to lowercase.)

9. Apply the Title style to the title *Equipment Rental Agreement* and apply the Heading 1 style to the headings in the document: *Lease, Rent, Use and Operation of Equipment, Insurance, Risk of Loss, Maintenance, Return of Equipment, Warranties of Lessee, Default*, and *Further Assurances*.

10. Apply the Centered style set.

11. Apply your custom document theme to the document.

12. Insert the Sample 1 watermark building block.

13. Insert the Banded footer building block.

14. Delete the two entries you made at the AutoCorrect dialog box.

15. Save, print, and then close **U1-MRCForm.docx**.

16. At a blank document, delete the custom theme colors, custom theme fonts, and custom document theme named with your initials.

Figure WB-U1.3 Assessment 8

Upon the occurrence of default, mrc may, without any further notice, exercise any one or more of the following remedies:

   a) terminate this erag as to any or all items of Equipment;

   b) cause Lessee at its expense to promptly return the Equipment to mrc in the condition set forth in this erag;

   c) use, hold, sell, lease, or otherwise dispose of the Equipment or any item of it on the premises of Lessee or any other location without affecting the obligations of Lessee as provided in this erag;

   d) proceed by appropriate action either at law or in equity to enforce performance by Lessee of the applicable covenants of this erag or to recover damages for the breach of them; or

   e) exercise any other rights accruing to mrc under any applicable law upon a default by Lessee.

Assessment 9

Data Files

Create and Run Macros

1. Open a blank document and then create the following macros:
   a. Create a macro named *XXXAPMFormat* (use your initials in place of the *XXX*) that changes the top margin to 1.5 inches and then selects the entire document and changes the font to Candara.
   b. Create a macro named *XXXAPMSubtitle* that is assigned to the keyboard command Alt + S that selects the line (press the F8 function key and then press the End key), changes the font size to 12 points, applies bold formatting, centers the text, and applies Blue, Accent 1, Lighter 80% paragraph shading (fifth column, second row in the *Theme Colors* section).
2. After recording the macros, close the document without saving it.
3. Open **Lease.docx** and then save it with the name **U1-Lease**.
4. Run the XXXAPMFormat macro.
5. Move the insertion point to the beginning of the heading *RENT* and then press Alt + S to run the XXXAPMSubtitle macro.
6. Run the XXXAPMSubtitle macro (using Alt + S) for the remaining headings: *DAMAGE DEPOSIT, USE OF PREMISES, CONDITION OF PREMISES, ALTERATIONS AND IMPROVEMENTS, NON-DELIVERY OF POSSESSION,* and *UTILITIES.*
7. Save, print, and then close **U1-Lease.docx**.
8. Open **REAgrmnt.docx** and then save it with the name **U1-REAgrmnt**.
9. Run the XXXAPMFormat macro.
10. Run the XXXAPMSubtitle macro (using Alt + S) for each heading in the document: *Financing, New Financing, Closing Costs, Survey,* and *Attorney Fees.*
11. Save, print, and then close **U1-REAgrmnt.docx**.
12. Delete the macros you created in this assessment: XXXAPMFormat and XXXAPMSubtitle.

Writing Activities

Create Building Blocks and Compose a Letter

You are the executive assistant to the director of the Human Resources Department at Clearline Manufacturing. You are responsible for preparing employee documents, notices, reports, and forms. You decide to create building blocks to increase the efficiency of and consistency in department documents. Press Ctrl + N to open a blank document and then save the document as a template named **CMTemplate** in your WL2U1 folder. Close the template document. Use File Explorer to open a blank document based on **CMTemplate.dotx**. At the blank document based on the template, create the following building blocks:

- Create a letterhead that includes the company name and any other enhancements to improve the appearance. Save the letterhead text as a building block.

- Create a building block footer that inserts the company address and telephone number. (You determine the address and telephone number.) Include a visual element in the footer, such as a border.

- You send documents to the board of directors and so you decide to include the board members' names and addresses as building blocks:

Mrs. Nancy Logan	Mr. Dion Jarvis
12301 132nd Avenue East	567 Federal Street
Warminster, PA 18974	Philadelphia, PA 19093

Dr. Austin Svoboda
9823 South 112th Street
Norristown, PA 18974

- Create a complimentary close building block that includes *Sincerely yours,* your name, and the title *Executive Assistant*.

At a blank document, write the body of a letter to a member of the board of directors and include at least the following information:

- Explain that the director of the Human Resources Department has created a new employee handbook and that it will be made available to all new employees. Also mention that the attorney for Clearline Manufacturing has reviewed the handbook and approved its content.

- Open **CMHandbook.docx** and then use the headings to summarize the contents of the handbook in a paragraph in the letter. Explain in the letter that a draft of the handbook is enclosed.

- Include any additional information you feel the directors may want to know.

Save the body of the letter as a separate document named CMLtr and then close **CMLtr.docx**. Use File Explorer to open a blank document based on **CMTemplate.dotx**. Using the building blocks you created, along with **CMLtr.docx**, create individual (opening a blank document each time based on **CMTemplate.dotx**) letters to Nancy Logan, Dion Jarvis, and Austin Svoboda. Save the letters individually and then print and close them.

Create a Custom Theme

Create a custom document theme for formatting documents that includes the colors and/or fonts you chose for the Clearline Manufacturing letterhead. Open the document **CMHandbook.docx** and then save the document and name it **U1-CMHandbook**. Apply at least the following formatting to the document:

- A table of contents building block
- A cover page building block
- A draft watermark building block
- Formatting to the title, headings, and subheadings
- Any additional formatting that improves the appearance and readability of the document

Select the text *(Click to display Longevity Schedule.)* at the end of the first paragraph in the section *Longevity Pay* and insert a hyperlink to the Excel file **CMPaySchedule.xlsx**. After inserting the hyperlink, click the hyperlink and make sure the Clearline worksheet displays and then close Excel.

Save, print, and then close **U1-CMHandbook.docx**. Delete the custom themes you created.

Internet Research

Prepare Information on Printer Specifications

You are responsible for purchasing new color laser printers for the Human Resources Department at Clearline Manufacturing. First, you need to research printers and prepare a report about them to the director of the department. Using the Internet, search for at least two companies that produce color laser printers. Determine information such as printer make and model, printer performance, printer cost, and prices for printer cartridges. Using the information you find, prepare a report to the director, Deana Terril. Type at least one list in the report and then create and apply a customized bullet to the list. Insert a predesigned header or footer and create and apply a custom theme to the report. Save the document and name it **U1-Printers**. Print and then close **U1-Printers.docx**.

Microsoft®

Word Level 2

Unit 2

Formatting and Customizing Documents

Inserting Special Features and References

> Study Tools

Study tools include a presentation and a list of chapter Quick Steps and Hint margin notes. Use these resources to help you further develop and review skills learned in this chapter.

> Concepts Check

Check your understanding by identifying application tools used in this chapter. If you are a SNAP user, launch the Concepts Check from your Assignments page.

> Recheck

Check your understanding by taking this quiz. If you are a SNAP user, launch the Recheck from your Assignments page.

Skills Exercise

Additional activities are available to SNAP users. If you are a SNAP user, access these activities from your Assignments page.

Skills Assessment

Assessment 1

Sort Text

> Data Files

1. Open **SFSSorting.docx** and then save it with the name **5-SFSSorting**.
2. Select the nine lines of text below the heading *Executive Team* and then sort the text alphabetically by last name.
3. Sort the three columns of text below the title *New Employees* by date of hire in ascending order.
4. Sort the text in the *First Qtr.* column in the table numerically in descending order.
5. Save, print, and then close **5-SFSSorting.docx**.

Assessment 2

Insert Footnotes in Designing a Newsletter Report

> Data Files

1. Open **DesignNwsltr.docx** and then save it with the name **5-DesignNwsltr**.
2. Create the first footnote shown in Figure WB-5.1 at the end of the first paragraph in the *Applying Guidelines* section.
3. Create the second footnote shown in the figure at the end of the third paragraph in the *Applying Guidelines* section.
4. Create the third footnote shown in the figure at the end of the last paragraph in the *Applying Guidelines* section.
5. Create the fourth footnote shown in the figure at the end of the only paragraph in the *Choosing Paper Size and Type* section.
6. Create the fifth footnote shown in the figure at the end of the only paragraph in the *Choosing Paper Weight* section.
7. Save and then print **5-DesignNwsltr.docx**.
8. Select the entire document and then change the font to Constantia.

9. Select all the footnotes and then change the font to Constantia.
10. Delete the third footnote *(Maddock)*.
11. Save, print, and then close **5-DesignNwsltr.docx**.

Figure WB-5.1 Assessment 2

James Haberman, "Designing a Newsletter," *Desktop Designs* (2018): 23-29.

Shirley Pilante, "Adding Pizzazz to Your Newsletter," *Desktop Publisher* (2017): 32-39.

Arlita Maddock, "Guidelines for a Better Newsletter," *Business Computing* (2018): 9-14.

Monica Alverso, "Paper Styles for Newsletters," *Design Technologies* (2018): 45-51.

Keith Sutton, "Choosing Paper Styles," *Design Techniques* (2018): 8-11.

Assessment 3

Data Files

Insert Sources and Citations in a Privacy Rights Report

1. Open **PrivRights.docx** and then save it with the name **5-PrivRights**.
2. Make sure that MLA style is selected in the Citations & Bibliography group on the References tab.
3. Format the title page to meet MLA requirements with the following changes:
   a. Select the entire document, change the font to 12-point Cambria, change the line spacing to double spacing, and then remove the extra spacing after paragraphs.
   b. Move the insertion point to the beginning of the document, type your name, press the Enter key, type your instructor's name, press the Enter key, type your course title, press the Enter key, type the current date, and then press the Enter key.
   c. Type the title Privacy Rights and then center it.
   d. Insert a header that displays your last name and the page number at the right margin and then change the font to 12-point Cambria.
4. Press Ctrl + End to move the insertion point to the end of the document and then type the text shown in Figure WB-5.2 up to the first citation—the text *(Hartley)*. Insert the source information for a journal article written by Kenneth Hartley using the following information:

Author	Kenneth Hartley
Title	Privacy Laws
Journal Name	Business World
Year	2018
Pages	24-46
Volume	7

5. Continue typing the text up to the next citation—the text *(Ferraro)*—and insert the following source information for a book:

Author	Ramona Ferraro
Title	Business Employee Rights
Year	2018
City	Tallahassee
Publisher	Everglades

6. Continue typing the text up to the next citation—the text *(Aldrich)*—and insert the following information for an article in a periodical:

Author	Kelly Aldrich
Title	What Rights Do Employees Have?
Periodical Title	Great Plains Times
Year	2018
Month	May
Day	6
Pages	18-22

7. Insert page number 20 in the Kelly Aldrich quote citation using the Edit Citation dialog box.

8. Type the remaining text shown in Figure WB-5.2.

9. Edit the Kenneth Hartley source title to read *Small Business Privacy Laws* in the *Master List* section at the Source Manager dialog box (update both the Master List and the Current List).

10. Select and delete the last two sentences in the second paragraph and then delete the Ramona Ferraro source in the *Current List* section at the Source Manager dialog box.

11. Insert a works cited page on a separate page at the end of the document.

12. Create a new source in the document using options at the Source Manager dialog box and include the following source information for a website:

Author	Harold Davidson
Name of Web Page	Small Business Policies and Procedures
Year	2017
Month	December
Day	12
Year Accessed	2018
Month Accessed	February
Day Accessed	23
URL	www.emcp.net/policies

13. Insert a citation for Harold Davidson at the end of the last sentence in the first paragraph.

14. Update the works cited page.

15. Format the works cited page to meet MLA requirements by making the following changes:

    a. Select the heading *Works Cited* and all the entries and then click the *No Spacing* style thumbnail.

    b. Change the font to 12-point Cambria and then change the line spacing to double spacing.

    c. Center the title *Works Cited*.

    d. Format the works cited entries with a hanging indent.

16. Save and then print **5-PrivRights.docx**.

17. Change the document and works cited page from MLA style to APA style. Make sure you change the title of the sources list to *References*, select the references in the list and then remove the extra spacing after paragraphs, change the line spacing to double spacing, and change the font to 12-point Cambria.

18. Save, print page 2, and then close **5-PrivRights.docx**.

A company can sometimes make an exception to its policy for monitoring employees. If the company has pledged to respect any aspect of employee privacy, it must keep that pledge. For example, if a business states that it will not monitor employee email or phone calls, by law, it must follow this stated policy (Hartley). However, no legal requirement exists mandating that companies notify their employees when and if monitoring takes place (Ferraro). Therefore, employees should assume they are always monitored and act accordingly.

Privacy advocates are calling for this situation to change. "They acknowledge that employers have the right to ensure that their employees are doing their jobs, but they question the need to monitor employees without warning and without limit" (Aldrich 20). The American Civil Liberties Union has, in fact, proposed a Fair Electronic Monitoring Policy to prevent abuses of employee privacy.

Visual Benchmark

Data Files

Format a Report in MLA Style

1. Open **SecurityDefenses.docx** and then save it with the name **5-SecurityDefenses**.
2. Format the document so it displays as shown in Figure WB-5.3 with the following specifications:
   a. Change the document font to 12-point Cambria.
   b. Use the information from the works cited page to insert citations in the document text. The Hollingsworth citation is for a journal article, the Montoya citation is for a book, and the Gillespie citation is for a website.
   c. Format the works cited page to meet MLA requirements.
3. Save, print, and then close **5-SecurityDefenses.docx**.

Figure WB-5.3 Visual Benchmark

Last Name 3

Works Cited

Gillespie, Julietta. *Creating Computer Security Systems*. 21 August 2018. 8 September 2018.

   <www.emcp.net/publishing>.

Hollingsworth, Melanie. "Securing Vital Company Data." *Corporate Data Management*

   (2018): 8-11.

Montoya, Paul. *Designing and Building Secure Systems*. San Francisco: Golden Gate

   Publishing House, 2017.

Page 3

Last Name 2

   More and more people are using software products that deal with both viruses and
spyware in one package. Some can be set to protect your computer in real time, meaning
that they detect an incoming threat, alert you, and stop it before it is downloaded to your
computer. In addition to using antivirus and antispyware software, consider allowing
regular updates to your operating system. Companies release periodic updates that
address flaws in their shipped software or new threats that have come on the scene since
their software shipped (Hollingsworth).

Page 2

Last Name 1

Student Name
Instructor Name
Course Title
Current Date

Security Defenses

   Whether protecting a large business or your personal laptop, certain security
defenses are available that help prevent attacks and avoid data loss, including firewalls and
software that detects and removes malware.

   A firewall is a part of your computer system that blocks unauthorized access to your
computer or network even as it allows authorized access. You can create firewalls using
software, hardware, or a combination of software and hardware (Hollingsworth). Firewalls
are like guards at the gate of the Internet. Messages that come into or leave a computer or
network go through the firewall, where they are inspected. Any message that does not meet
preset criteria for security is blocked. "You can set up trust levels that allow some types of
communications through and block others, or designate specific sources of
communications that should be allowed access" (Montoya 15).

   All computer users should consider using antivirus and antispyware software to
protect their computers, data, and privacy. Antivirus products require that you update the
virus definitions on a regular basis to ensure that you have protection from new viruses as
they are introduced. Once you have updated definitions, you run a scan and have several
options: to quarantine viruses to keep your system safe from them, to delete a virus
completely, and to report viruses to the antivirus manufacturer to help keep their
definitions current. Antispyware performs a similar function regarding spyware (Gillespie).

Page 1

Case Study

Lincoln Freelance Services provides freelance employees for businesses in Baltimore and the surrounding communities. A new industrial park has opened in Baltimore and a number of temporary positions need to be filled. As the office manager for Lincoln Freelance Services, you decide to send a letter to current clients living in Baltimore to let them know about the new industrial park and the temporary jobs available. Create a letter main document and include the information that a new industrial park is opening in a few months (provide the location, which you should determine) and that Lincoln Freelance Services is providing temporary employees for many of the technology jobs. Include a list of at least five technology jobs (find job titles on the Internet) for which you will be placing employees. Include any additional information in the letter that you feel is important. Merge the letter main document with only those clients in the **LFSClients.mdb** data source file that live in Baltimore. Save the merged letters and name the document **5-LFSLtrs**. Print and then close **5-LFSLtrs.docx**. Save the letter main document and name it **5-LFSMD** and then close the document.

Your supervisor at Lincoln Freelance Services has given you a report on newsletter guidelines and asked you to reformat it using the APA reference style. Open **5-DesignNwsltr.docx** and then save it with the name **5-DesignNwsltr-APA**. Remove the title *CREATING NEWSLETTER LAYOUT* and change the spacing before the heading *Choosing Paper Size and Type* to 6 points. Remove the footnotes and insert the information as in-text journal citations and then add a references page on a separate page. Center the title *References* and change the font to uppercase. Select the entire document and change the font to Cambria. Save **5-DesignNwsltr-APA.docx**.

Your supervisor at Lincoln Freelance Services has asked you to include some additional information on newsletter guidelines. Using the Internet, look for websites that provide information on desktop publishing and/or newsletter design. Include in the **5-DesignNwsltr-APA.docx** report at least one additional paragraph with information you found on the Internet and include a citation for each source from which you have borrowed information. Save, print, and then close the report.

Creating Specialized Tables and Indexes

CHAPTER 6

Study tools include a presentation and a list of chapter Quick Steps and Hint margin notes. Use these resources to help you further develop and review skills learned in this chapter.

Concepts Check

Check your understanding by identifying application tools used in this chapter. If you are a SNAP user, launch the Concepts Check from your Assignments page.

Recheck

Check your understanding by taking this quiz. If you are a SNAP user, launch the Recheck from your Assignments page.

Skills Exercise

Additional activities are available to SNAP users. If you are a SNAP user, access these activities from your Assignments page.

Skills Assessment

Assessment 1

Data Files

Create and Update a Table of Contents for a Photography Report

1. Open **PhotoRpt.docx** and then save it with the name **6-PhotoRpt**.
2. Move the insertion point to the beginning of the heading *Photography* and then insert a section break that begins a new page.
3. With the insertion point positioned below the section break, insert page numbers at the bottom center of each page and change the beginning number to 1.
4. Press Ctrl + Home to move the insertion point to the beginning of the document (on the blank page) and then create a table of contents with the *Automatic Table 1* option at the Table of Contents button drop-down list.
5. Display the Table of Contents dialog box, change the *Formats* option to *Distinctive*, and make sure a 3 displays in the *Show levels* measurement box.
6. Change the page number format on the table of contents page to lowercase roman numerals.
7. Save the document and then print only the table of contents page.
8. Insert a page break at the beginning of the heading *Camera Basics*.
9. Update the table of contents.
10. Save the document and then print only the table of contents page.
11. Close **6-PhotoRpt.docx**.

Assessment 2

Data Files

Insert Captions and a Table of Figures in a Report

1. Open **InputDevices.docx** and then save it with the name **6-InputDevices**.
2. Insert a caption for each of the three images in the document that uses *Figure* as the label, uses numbers (1, 2, 3, and so on) as the figure numbers, displays centered, and below the image. Use *Keyboard* for the first figure caption, *Mouse* for the second, and *Laptop* for the third.
3. Move the insertion point to the beginning of the title COMPUTER INPUT DEVICES and then insert a section break that begins a new page.
4. Press Ctrl + Home, type Table of Figures, press the Enter key, and then insert a table of figures with the Formal format.
5. Apply the Heading 1 style to the title *Table of Figures*.
6. Move the insertion point to the title COMPUTER INPUT DEVICES. Insert a page number at the bottom center of each page and change the starting number to 1.
7. Move the insertion point to the title TABLE OF FIGURES and then change the page numbering style to lowercase roman numerals.
8. Insert a page break at the beginning of the heading MOUSE.
9. Update the table of figures.
10. Save, print, and then close **6-InputDevices.docx**.

Assessment 3

Data Files

Create and Update an Index for a Newsletter

1. At a blank document, create the text shown in Figure WB-6.1 as a concordance file and then save the document and name it **6-ConFile**.
2. Print and then close **6-ConFile.docx**.
3. Open **DesignNwsltr.docx** and then save it with the name **6-DesignNwsltr**.
4. Make the following changes to the document:
   a. Mark the text for an index using the concordance file **6-ConFile.docx**.
   b. Move the insertion point to the end of the document, insert a page break, type INDEX, press the Enter key, and then insert the index with the Classic format.
   c. Apply the Heading 1 style to the index title.
5. Number pages at the bottom center of each page.
6. Change the line spacing to double spacing for the entire document.
7. Insert a page break at the beginning of the title CREATING NEWSLETTER LAYOUT.
8. Update the index. (The index returns to the default line spacing.)
9. Save the document and then print the index page only.
10. Close **6-DesignNwsltr.docx**.

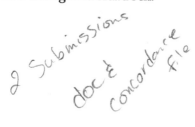

Figure WB-6.1 Assessment 3

NEWSLETTER	Newsletter
newsletter	Newsletter
consistency	Newsletter: consistency
element	Elements
margins	Elements: margins
column layout	Elements: column layout
nameplate	Elements: nameplate
location	Elements: location
logos	Elements: logos
color	Elements: color
ruled lines	Elements: ruled lines
Focus	Elements: focus
focus	Elements: focus
balance	Elements: balance
graphics	Graphics
images	Images
photos	Photos
Headlines	Newsletter: headlines
headlines	Newsletter: headlines
subheads	Newsletter: subheads
White space	White space
white space	White space
directional flow	Newsletter: directional flow
paper	Paper
Size	Paper: size
type	Paper: type
weight	Paper: weight
stock	Paper: stock
margin size	Newsletter: margin size

Assessment
4

Customize an Index

1. You can customize an index with options at the Index dialog box. At a blank document, display this dialog box by clicking the References tab and then clicking the Insert Index button in the Index group. Look at the options offered at the dialog box and determine how to change the leader style and number of columns. Close the dialog box and then close the blank document.
2. Open **6-DesignNwsltr.docx** and then save it with the name **6-Newsletter**.
3. Make the following changes to the index:
   a. Display the Index dialog box.
   b. Change to a format that contains leaders.
   c. Change the leaders to hyphens (rather than periods).
   d. Specify three columns.
   e. Close the Index dialog box. When asked if you want to replace the selected index, click OK.
4. Save **6-Newsletter.docx**.
5. Print only the index and then close the document.

Visual Benchmark

Create a Table of Contents and Table of Figures

1. Open **Networks.docx** and then save it with the name **6-Networks**.
2. Format the document so it appears as shown in Figure WB-6.2 with the following specifications:
   a. Insert the captions for the figures as shown (see Page 3 of the figure).
   b. Insert the table of contents as shown (see Page 1 of the figure) using the *From template* format option with hyphen leaders.
   c. Insert the table of figures as shown (see Page 2 of the figure) using the *From template* format option with period leaders.
   d. Insert page numbers at the right margins as shown (see Pages 2 and 4 of the figure).
3. Save, print, and then close **6-Networks.docx**.

Figure WB-6.2 Visual Benchmark

TABLE OF CONTENTS

Page 1

FIGURES

ii

Page 2

continues

Figure WB-6.2 Visual Benchmark—*Continued*

COMMUNICATIONS SYSTEMS

A computer network is one kind of communications system. This system includes sending and receiving hardware, transmission and relay systems, common sets of standards so all the equipment can "talk" to each other, and communications software.

NETWORK COMMUNICATIONS

You use such a networked communications system whenever you send/receive IM or email messages, pay a bill online, shop at an Internet store, send a document to a shared printer at work or at home, or download a file.

The world of computer network communications systems is made up of:

- Transmission media upon which the data travels to/from its destination.
- A set of standards and network protocols (rules for how data is handled as it travels along a communications channel). Devices use these to send and receive data to and from each other.
- Hardware and software to connect to a communications pathway from the sending and receiving ends.

Figure 1 Wireless Network Base

The first step in understanding a communications system is to learn the basics about transmission signals and transmission speeds when communicating over a network.

TYPES OF SIGNALS

Two types of signals are used to transmit voices and other sounds over a computer network: analog and digital. An analog signal is formed by continuous sound waves that fluctuate from high to low. Your voice is transmitted as an analog signal over traditional telephone lines at a certain frequency. A digital signal uses a discrete signal that is either high or low. In computer terms, high represents the digital bit 1, and low represents the digital bit 0. These are the only two states for digital data.

Telephone lines carry your voice using an analog signal. However, computers don't "speak" analog;

Figure 2 Computer Modem

rather, they use a binary system of 1s and 0s to turn analog data into digital signals. If you send data between computers using an analog medium such as a phone line, the signal has to be transformed from digital to analog (modulated) and back again to digital (demodulated) to be understood by the

1

at sends and receives data from a transmission
nnection is a modem. The word modem comes
dulate.

se a digital signal, saving the trouble of
demise in 2009 of analog television
Many people were sent scrambling to either
digital transmissions back to analog to work
too, use a pure digital signal method of sending

2

Page 3

Page 4

Case Study

Part

1

Data Files

You work in the Human Resources Department at Brennan Distributors and are responsible for preparing an employee handbook. Open **BDEmpHandbook.docx** and then save it with the name **6-BDEmpHandbook**. Apply the following specifications to the document:

- Insert a page break before each centered title (except the first title, *Introduction*).
- Apply the Heading 1 style to the titles and the Heading 2 style to the headings.
- Change to a style set of your choosing.
- Apply a theme that makes the handbook easy to read.
- Insert a table of contents.
- Create a concordance file with a minimum of 10 entries. (You determine the entries.) Save the concordance file with the name **6-BDEmpConFile**. Insert an index.
- Insert appropriate page numbering. ***Hint: Insert a* Next Page *section break at the beginning of the* INTRODUCTION *heading.***
- Insert a cover page and insert the appropriate text in the placeholders. Delete any extra placeholders.
- Add any other elements to improve the appearance of the document.

Save, print, and then close **6-BDEmpHandbook.docx**.

Part

2

Data Files

Open **NavigateWeb.docx** and then save it with the name **6-NavigateWeb**. Apply the following specifications to the document:

- Move the insertion point to any cell in the first table and then use the caption feature to create the caption *Table 1: Common Top-Level Domain Suffixes* that displays above the table.
- Move the insertion point to any cell in the second table and then create the caption *Table 2: Common Search Tools*.
- Move the insertion point to any cell in the third table and then create the caption *Table 3: Advanced Search Parameters*.
- Insert a table of contents.
- Insert a table of figures on the page following the table of contents.
- Insert appropriate page numbering.
- Check the page breaks in the document. If a heading displays at the bottom of a page and the paragraph of text that follows displays at the top of the next page, format the heading so it stays with the paragraph. ***Hint: Do this at the Paragraph dialog box with the Line and Page Breaks tab selected.***
- If necessary, update the table of contents and the table of figures.

Save, print, and then close **6-NavigateWeb.docx**.

Part

3

Send an email to your instructor detailing the steps you followed to create table captions. Attach **6-NavigateWeb.docx** to the email.

Working with Shared Documents

Study tools include a presentation and a list of chapter Quick Steps and Hint margin notes. Use these resources to help you further develop and review skills learned in this chapter.

Concepts Check

Check your understanding by identifying application tools used in this chapter. If you are a SNAP user, launch the Concepts Check from your Assignments page.

Recheck

Check your understanding by taking this quiz. If you are a SNAP user, launch the Recheck from your Assignments page.

Skills Exercise

Additional activities are available to SNAP users. If you are a SNAP user, access these activities from your Assignments page.

Skills Assessment

Assessment

1

Data Files

Insert Comments in a Web Report

1. Open **NavigateWeb.docx** and then save it with the name **7-NavigateWeb**.
2. Delete the only comment in the document.
3. Position the insertion point at the end of the first paragraph in the section *IPs and URLs* and then insert a comment with the following text: *Please identify what the letters ICANN stand for.*
4. Position the insertion point at the end of the third paragraph in the section *IPs and URLs* and then insert a comment with the following text: *Insert a caption for the following table and the two other tables in the document.*
5. Position the insertion point at the end of the last paragraph in the document (above the table) and insert a comment with the following text: *Include in the following table additional examples of methods for narrowing a search.*
6. Save the document and then print only the comments.
7. Close **7-NavigateWeb.docx**.

Assessment

2

Data Files

Track Changes in a Computer Viruses Report

1. Open **CompChapters.docx** and then save it with the name **7-CompChapters**.
2. Turn on Track Changes and then make the following changes:
   a. Edit the first sentence in the document so it displays as follows: *The computer virus is one of the most familiar forms of risk to computer security.*
   b. Type computer's between *the* and *motherboard* in the last sentence in the first paragraph of the document.
   c. Delete the word *real* in the second sentence in the section *Types of Viruses* and then type significant.

d. Select and then delete the last sentence in the section *Methods of Virus Operation* (which begins *A well-known example of the logic bomb was the*).
　　　e. Turn off Track Changes.
　　3. Display the Word Options dialog box with *General* selected and then change the user name to *Stanley Phillips* and the initials to *SP*. Insert a check mark in the *Always use these values regardless of sign in to Office* check box.
　　4. Turn on Track Changes and then make the following changes:
　　　a. Delete the words *or cracker* in the seventh sentence in the section *Types of Viruses*.
　　　b. Delete the word *garner* in the first sentence in the section *CHAPTER 2: SECURITY RISKS* and then type generate.
　　　c. Select and then move the section *Employee Theft* after the section *Cracking Software for Copying*.
　　　d. Turn off Track Changes.
　　5. Display the Word Options dialog box with *General* selected. Change the user name back to the original name and the initials back to the original initials. Also remove the check mark from the *Always use these values regardless of sign in to Office* check box.
　　6. Print the document with the markups.
　　7. Accept all the changes in the document *except* the change moving the section *Employee Theft* after the section *Cracking Software for Copying*; reject this change.
　　8. Save, print, and then close **7-CompChapters.docx**.

Assessment 3

Compare Original and Revised Security Strategies Reports

1. Compare **Security.docx** with **EditedSecurity.docx** and insert the changes into a new document. *Hint: Choose* **New document** *at the expanded Compare Documents dialog box.*
2. Save the compared document and name it **7-Security**.
3. Print only the list of markups (not the document).
4. Reject the changes made to the bulleted text and the last paragraph in the *Disaster Recovery Plan* section and accept all the other changes.
5. Add a page number at the bottom center of each page.
6. Save the document, print only the document, and then close **7-Security.docx**.

Data Files

Assessment 4

Combine Original and Revised Legal Documents

1. Open **LegalSummons.docx** and then save it with the name **7-LegalSummons**.
2. Close **7-LegalSummons.docx**.
3. At a blank screen, combine **7-LegalSummons** (the original document) with **Review1-LegalSummons.docx** (the revised document) into the original document. *Hint: Choose* **Original document** *at the Combine Documents expanded dialog box.*
4. Accept all the changes in the document.
5. Save and then close **7-LegalSummons.docx**.
6. At a blank screen, combine **7-LegalSummons.docx** (the original document) with **Review2-LegalSummons.docx** (the revised document) into the original document.
7. Print only the list of markups.
8. Accept all the changes in the document.
9. Save, print, and then close **7-LegalSummons.docx**.

Data Files

Link an Excel Chart with a Word Document

1. Open **WESales.docx** and then save it with the name **7-WESales**.
2. Open Excel and then open the workbook **WESales.xlsx**.
3. Save the Excel workbook with the name **7-WESales**.
4. Link the Excel chart to the end of **7-WESales.docx**. (Make sure to use the Paste Special dialog box.)
5. Move the insertion point to the end of the document and then press the Enter key three times.
6. Make **7-WESales.xlsx** active, select the text in the first cell (the company name and address), copy the selected text, and then paste it as unformatted text at the end of **7-WESales.docx**. (Make sure to use the Paste Special dialog box.)
7. Save, print, and then close **7-WESales.docx**.
8. With Excel active, make the following changes to the data in the specified cells:
   a. Change the amount in cell F4 from *$500,750* to *$480,200*.
   b. Change the amount in cell E5 from *$410,479* to *$475,500*.
9. Save and close **7-WESales.xlsx** and then close Excel.
10. Open **7-WESales.docx** and click Yes at the message asking if you want to update the document.
11. Save, print, and then close **7-WESales.docx**.

Track Changes in a Table

1. Open **SalesTable.docx** and then save it with the name **7-SalesTable**.
2. Display the Advanced Track Changes Options dialog box, look at the options for customizing tracked changes in a table, and then make the following changes:
   a. Change the color for inserted cells to Light Purple.
   b. Change the color for deleted cells to Light Green.
3. Turn on Track Changes and then make the following changes:
   a. Insert a new row at the beginning of the table.
   b. Merge the cells in the new row. (At the message stating that the action will not be marked as a change, click OK.)
   c. Type Clearline Manufacturing in the merged cell.
   d. Delete the *Fanning, Andrew* row.
   e. Insert a new row below *Barnet, Jacqueline* and then type Montano, Neil in the first cell, $530,678 in the second cell, and $550,377 in the third cell.
   f. Turn off Track Changes.
4. Save and then print the document with markups.
5. Accept all the changes.
6. Display the Advanced Track Changes Options dialog box and then return the color of the inserted cells to Light Blue and the color of the deleted cells to Pink.
7. Save, print, and then close **7-SalesTable.docx**.

Visual Benchmark

Track Changes in an Employee Performance Document

1. Open **NSSEmpPerf.docx** and then save it with the name **7-NSSEmpPerf**.
2. Turn on Track Changes and then make the changes shown in Figure WB-7.1. (Make the editing changes before moving the *Employment Records* section after the *Performance Evaluation* section.)
3. Turn off Track Changes and then print only the list of markups.
4. Accept all the changes to the document.
5. Save, print, and then close **7-NSSEmpPerf.docx**.
6. At a blank screen, combine **7-NSSEmpPerf.docx** (the original document) with **EditedNSSEmpPerf.docx** (the revised document) into the original document.
7. Accept all the changes to the document.
8. Save, print, and then close **7-NSSEmpPerf.docx**.

Figure WB-7.1 Visual Benchmark

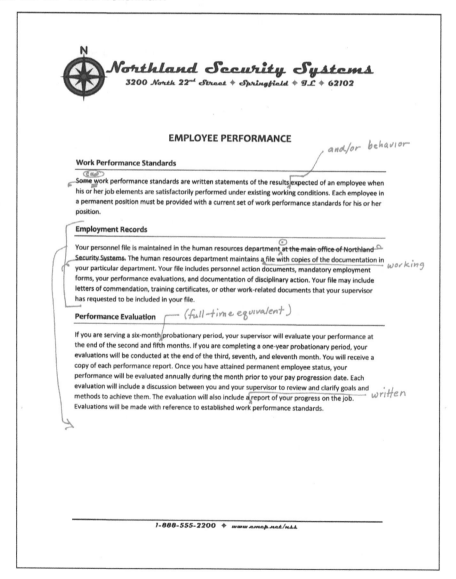

Case Study

Part 1

You work in the Training Department at Hart International. Your department is responsible for preparing training materials and training employees on how to use software applications within the company. Your supervisor, Nicole Sweeney, has asked you to help her prepare a Microsoft Word training manual. She has written a portion of the manual and has had another employee, Gina Singh, review the contents using the Track Changes feature. Nicole has asked you to combine Gina's revised version with the original document. To do this, combine **HITraining.docx** with **HITrainingGS.docx**. Go through the original document with the tracked changes and accept and/or reject each revision. Not all of Gina's changes are correct, so check each one before accepting or rejecting it. Save the combined document and name it **7-HITraining**.

Part 2

Your supervisor at Hart International, Nicole Sweeney, has asked you to prepare training materials on how to check the spelling and grammar in a document and how to display readability statistics after the spelling and grammar check is complete. Using **7-HITraining.docx** as a guideline, write information (including steps) on how to complete a spelling and grammar check in a document and how to turn on the display of readability statistics. Include in the document a table that presents the names of the buttons available at the Spelling task pane and the Grammar task pane and a brief description of what task each button performs. Save the completed document and name it **7-HISpelling**.

Part 3

If possible, send a copy of the document you created in Part 2 to one or two classmates and have them edit it with Track Changes turned on. Combine their edited documents with your original **7-HISpelling** document. Save, print, and then close the document.

Part 4

Open **7-HITraining.docx**, move the insertion point to the end of the document, and then insert **7-HISpelling.docx**. Apply at least the following elements to the document:

- Heading styles
- Style set
- Theme
- Table styles
- Table of contents
- Page numbering
- Cover page

Save, print, and then close the document.

Protecting and Preparing Documents

Study Tools

Study tools include a presentation and a list of chapter Quick Steps and Hint margin notes. Use these resources to help you further develop and review skills learned in this chapter.

Concepts Check

Check your understanding by identifying application tools used in this chapter. If you are a SNAP user, launch the Concepts Check from your Assignments page.

Recheck

Check your understanding by taking this quiz. If you are a SNAP user, launch the Recheck from your Assignments page.

Skills Exercise

Additional activities are available to SNAP users. If you are a SNAP user, access these activities from your Assignments page.

Skills Assessment

Assessment

1

Data Files

Restrict Formatting and Editing of a Writing Report

1. Open **WritingProcess.docx** and then save it with the name **8-WritingProcess**.
2. Display the Restrict Editing task pane and then restrict formatting to the Heading 2 and Heading 3 styles. (At the message asking about removing formatting or styles that are not allowed, click No.)
3. Enforce the protection and include the password *writing*.
4. Click the Available styles hyperlink.
5. Apply the Heading 2 style to the two titles *THE WRITING PROCESS* and *REFERENCES*.
6. Apply the Heading 3 style to the seven remaining headings in the document. (The Heading 3 style may not display until the Heading 2 style is applied to the first title.)
7. Close the Styles task pane and then close the Restrict Editing task pane.
8. Save the document and then print only page 1.
9. Close **8-WritingProcess.docx**.

Assessment 2

Insert Comments in a Software Life Cycle Document

Data Files

1. Open **CommCycle.docx** and then save it with the name **8-CommCycle**.
2. Display the Restrict Editing task pane, restrict editing to comments only, and then start enforcing the protection. (Do not include a password.)
3. At the end of the first paragraph in the document, type the comment Create a SmartArt graphic that illustrates the software life cycle.
4. At the end of the paragraph in the *Design* section, type the comment Include the problem-solving steps.
5. At the end of the paragraph in the *Testing* section, type the comment Describe a typical beta testing cycle.
6. Print only the comments.
7. Close the Restrict Editing task pane.
8. Save and then close **8-CommCycle.docx**.

Assessment 3

Insert Document Properties, Check Compatibility, and Save a Presentation Document in a Different Format

Data Files

1. Open **Presentation.docx** and then save it with the name **8-Presentation**.
2. Make the following changes to the document:
   a. Apply the Heading 1 style to the title *Delivering a How-To Presentation*.
   b. Apply the Heading 2 style to the three headings in the document.
   c. Change the style set to Centered.
   d. Apply the View theme and apply the Green theme colors.
   e. Change the color of the image to Green, Accent color 1 Light (second column, third row in the *Recolor* section).
3. Display the 8-Presentation.docx Properties dialog box with the Summary tab selected and then type the following in the specified text boxes:

Title	Delivering a How-To Presentation
Subject	Presentations
Author	(Type your first and last names)
Keywords	presentation, how-to, delivering, topics
Comments	This document describes the three steps involved in developing a how-to presentation.

4. Close the dialog box.
5. ~~Save **8-Presentation.docx** and then print only the document properties.~~ no
6. Run the Accessibility Checker on the document. Create alternate text for the image. Type the text Presentation image for the title and type Person giving a presentation. for the description. Create alternate text for the SmartArt graphic. Type the text Presentation SmartArt graphic for the title and type Three steps in developing a how-to presentation. for the description. Close the Format Shape task pane and then close the Accessibility Checker.
7. Save and then print **8-Presentation.docx**.
8. Run the Compatibility Checker to determine what features are not supported by earlier versions of Word.
9. Save the document in the *Word 97-2003 Document (*.doc)* format and name it **8-Presentation-2003format**.
10. Save and then close **8-Presentation-2003format.doc**.

Create a Document on Inserting and Removing a Signature

1. The Text group on the Insert tab contains a Signature Line button for inserting a signature in a document. Use Word's Help or Tell Me features to learn about inserting and removing a signature by typing add or remove a digital signature at the Word Help window and then clicking the <u>Add or remove a digital signature in Office files</u> hyperlink. Read the information in the article and then prepare a Word document with the following information:

   - An appropriate title
   - How to create a signature line in Word
   - How to sign a signature line in Word
   - How to remove a signature from Word
   - How to add an invisible digital signature in Word

2. Apply formatting to enhance the appearance of the document.
3. Save the document and name it **8-Signature**.
4. Print and then close **8-Signature.docx**.

Visual Benchmark

Data Files

Format a Document, Insert Document Properties, Check Compatibility, and Save a Document in a Different Format

1. Open **InfoSystem.docx** and then save it with the name **8-InfoSystem**.
2. Format the document so it appears as shown in Figure WB-8.1 with the following specifications:
   a. Apply the Lines (Stylish) style set and then apply the Dividend theme.
   b. Insert the Integral footer and then type your name as the author.
   c. Insert the SmartArt Continuous Cycle graphic and then apply the Colorful - Accent Colors color (first option in the *Colorful* section) and the Metallic Scene style.
   d. Recolor the image as shown in the figure.
   e. Make any other changes needed so your document displays as shown in Figure WB-8.1.
3. Display the 8-InfoSystem.docx Properties dialog box with the Summary tab selected and then type the following in the specified text boxes:

Title	Developing an Information System
Subject	Software Development
Author	(Type your first and last names)
Category	Software
Keywords	software, design, plan
Comments	This document describes the four steps involved in developing an information system.

4. Save the document and then print only the document properties.
5. Inspect the document and remove any hidden text.
6. Run the Accessibility Checker and then create alternate text for the image.
7. Run the Compatibility Checker to determine what features are not supported by earlier versions of Word.
8. Save the document in the *Word 97-2003 Document (*.doc)* format and name it **8-InfoSystem-2003format**.
9. Save, print, and then close **8-InfoSystem-2003format.doc**.

Figure WB-8.1 Visual Benchmark

Developing an Information System

Identifying and assembling a team of employees with the required skills and expertise is a necessary first step in developing a new in-house information system. A management group may be involved in answering questions and providing information in the early planning phases of the project, but programmers and/or software engineers handle the design and implementation of any new system.

Programmers specialize in the development of new software, while software engineers are highly skilled professionals with programming and teamwork training. Their organized, professional application of the software development process is called software engineering.

Project Plan

The first step in the system development life cycle is planning. The planning step involves preparing a needs analysis and conducting feasibility studies. During this step, a company usually establishes a project team, and the team creates a project plan. The project plan includes an estimate of how long the project will take to complete, an outline of the steps involved, and a list of deliverables. Deliverables are documents, services, hardware, and software that must be finished and delivered by a certain time and date.

Project Team

Because of their large size, information systems require the creation of a project team. A project team usually includes a project manager, who acts as the team leader. Sometimes the project manager also functions as a systems analyst, responsible for completing the systems analysis and making design recommendations. Other project team members include software engineers and technicians. The software engineers deal with programming software, while technicians handle hardware issues. The comprehensive process software engineers initiate is called the system development life cycle (SDLC), a series of steps culminating in a completed information system.

Designing the System

A project is ready to move into the design stage once the project team has approved the plan, including the budget. The design process begins with the writing of the documentation, which covers functional and design specifications. In most cases, the project team creates the functional specifications, describing what the system must be able to do.

Implementation

The project can move into the next phase, implementation, once the development team and the systems house develop the design specification and approve the plans. This step is where the actual work of putting the system together is completed, including creating a prototype and completing the programming. In most cases, implementing the new system is the longest, most difficult step in the process.

STUDENT NAM

Page 1

Support Stage

A system goes into the support stage after it has been accepted and approved. A support contract normally allows users to contact the systems house for technical support, training, and sometimes on-site troubleshooting. Even if the system was designed in-house, the responsible department often operates as an independent entity—sometimes even charging the department acquiring the system. The support stage continues until a new information system is proposed and developed, usually years later. At that point, the existing system is retired and no longer used.

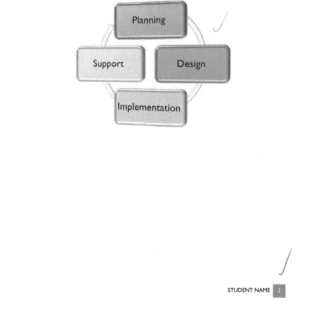

STUDENT NAME 2

Page 2

Case Study

You work in the Training Department at Hart International. Your department is responsible for preparing training materials and training employees on how to use software applications within the company. Your supervisor asked you to help her prepare a Microsoft Word training manual. She had already written part of the manual and had you add training information and then format the manual.

If you completed Part 1 of the Case Study for Chapter 7, you should have a document named **7-HITraining.docx** saved in your WL2C7 folder. Open **7-HITraining.docx** from the WL2C7 folder on your storage medium and then save the document in your WL2C8 folder and name it **8-HITraining**. Move the insertion point to the end of the document and then insert **HIManual.docx** from your WL2C8 folder. (Insert the file with the Object button in the Text group on the Insert tab.)

If **7-HITraining.docx** is not saved in your WL2C7 folder, open **HIManual.docx** from your WL2C8 folder and then save the document and name it **8-HITraining.docx**.

Add information to the document on how to insert the following buttons on the Quick Access Toolbar: Quick Print, Open, Close, Spelling & Grammar, and Thesaurus. Apply formatting to the document, update the table of contents, and then save the completed document.

Part

2

Your supervisor at Hart International has decided that the options on company computers should be modified. She wants you to determine the steps for making the modifications and then include the steps in the training manual. Open the Word Options dialog box and then determine how to make the following modifications:

- Change the Office background to Geometry and the Office theme to Dark Gray. *Hint: These options are in the* **General** *option.*
- Turn on the display of readability statistics. *Hint: These options are in the* **Proofing** *option.*
- Change the minutes for saving AutoRecover information to 5 minutes. *Hint: These options are in the* **Save** *option.*
- Change the number of documents that display in the *Recent* option list to 15 documents. *Hint: The option is in the* **Display** *section of the* **Advanced** *option in the Word Options dialog box. You will need to scroll down the dialog box to display this section.*

With **8-HITraining.docx** open, write the steps involved in making each customization listed above. If your document contains a table of contents, update the entire table. Save the document.

Part

3

Prepare the document for distribution by inspecting it and then restricting editing to comments only. Save, print, and then close **8-HITraining.docx**.

Microsoft® Word Level 2

Unit 2 Performance Assessment

Data Files

Before beginning unit work, copy the WL2U2 folder to your storage medium and then make WL2U2 the active folder.

Assessing Proficiency

In this unit, you learned how to use features for citing sources in a document, such as footnotes, endnotes, in-text citations, and bibliographies; how to insert tables of contents, tables of figures, and indexes; and how to use features for sharing and distributing documents, such as inserting comments, tracking changes, comparing and combining documents, linking and embedding files, and restricting access to documents.

Assessment

1

Data Files

Sort Text

1. Open **SHSSort.docx** and then save it with the name **U2-SHSSort**.
2. Select the five clinic names, addresses, and telephone numbers below the heading *SUMMIT HEALTH SERVICES* and then sort the text alphabetically in ascending order by clinic name.
3. Sort the three columns of text below the heading *EXECUTIVE TEAM* by the extension number in ascending order.
4. Sort the text in the table in the *First Half Expenses* column numerically in descending order.
5. Save, print, and then close **U2-SHSSort.docx**.

Assessment

2

Data Files

Select Records in a Data Source File and Create Mailing Labels

1. At a blank document, use the mail merge feature to create mailing labels with Avery US Letter, 5160 Easy Peel Address Labels and the **SHS.mdb** data source file (located in the WL2U2 folder). Before merging the data source file with the mailing labels document, sort the records alphabetically in ascending order by last name.
2. Merge the sorted data source file with the labels document.
3. Press Ctrl + A to select the entire merged labels document and then click the *No Spacing* style.
4. Save the merged labels document and name it **U2-Lbls1**.
5. Close the document and then close the labels main document without saving it.

6. Use the mail merge feature to create mailing labels using the **SHS.mdb** data source file. (Use the same label option as in Step 1.) Select records from the data source file of clients living in the city of Greensboro and then merge those records with the labels document. Apply the No Spacing style to the entire merged labels document.
7. Save the merged labels document and name it **U2-Lbls2**.
8. Close the document and then close the labels main document without saving it.

Assessment

3

Data Files

Insert Footnotes in a Desktop Publishing Report

1. Open **DTP.docx** and then save it with the name **U2-DTP**.
2. Insert the first footnote shown in Figure WB-U2.1 at the end of the second paragraph in the section *Defining Desktop Publishing*.
3. Insert the second footnote shown in the figure at the end of the fourth paragraph in the section *Defining Desktop Publishing*.
4. Insert the third footnote shown in the figure at the end of the second paragraph in the section *Planning the Publication*.
5. Insert the fourth footnote shown in the figure at the end of the last paragraph in the document.
6. Keep the heading *Planning the Publication* together with the paragraph of text that follows it.
7. Save and then print **U2-DTP.docx**.
8. Select the entire document and then change the font to Constantia.
9. Select all the footnotes and then change the font to Constantia.
10. Delete the third footnote.
11. Save, print, and then close **U2-DTP.docx**.

Figure WB-U2.1 Assessment 3

Laurie Fellers, *Desktop Publishing Design* (Dallas: Cornwall & Lewis, 2018), 67-72.

Joel Moriarity, "The Desktop Publishing Approach," *Desktop Publishing* (2018): 3-6.

Chun Man Wong, *Desktop Publishing with Style* (Seattle: Monroe-Ackerman, 2017), 89-93.

Andrew Rushton, *Desktop Publishing Tips and Tricks* (Minneapolis: Aurora, 2018), 103-106.

Assessment

4

Data Files

Create Citations and Prepare a Works Cited Page for a Report

1. Open **DesignWebsite.docx** and then save it with the name **U2-DesignWebsite**.
2. Format the title page to meet Modern Language Association (MLA) requirements with the following changes:
   a. Make sure the reference style for the document is set to MLA.
   b. Select the entire document, change the font to Cambria, change the font size to 12 points, change the line spacing to double spacing, and remove the extra space after paragraphs.

c. Move the insertion point to the beginning of the document, type your name, press the Enter key, type your instructor's name, press the Enter key, type your course title, press the Enter key, and then type the current date.

d. Insert a header that displays your last name and the page number at the right margin. Change the header font to Cambria and the font size to 12 points.

3. Press Ctrl + End to move the insertion point to the end of the document and then type the text shown in Figure WB-U2.2 (in MLA style) up to the first citation—the text *(Mercado)*. Insert the source information from a journal article written by Claudia Mercado using the following information:

Author	Claudia Mercado
Title	Connecting a Web Page
Journal Name	Connections
Year	2018
Pages	12-21
Volume	4

4. Continue typing the text up to the next citation—the text *(Holmes)*—and insert the following source information from a website:

Author	Brent Holmes
Name of Web Page	Hosting Your Web Page
Year	2017
Month	September
Day	28
Year Accessed	*(type current year)*
Month Accessed	*(type current month)*
Day Accessed	*(type current day)*
URL	www.emcp.net/webhosting

5. Continue typing the text up to the next citation—the text *(Vukovich)*—and insert the following information from a book:

Author	Ivan Vukovich
Title	Computer Technology in the Business Environment
Year	2018
City	San Francisco
Publisher	Gold Coast

6. Insert the page number in the citation by Ivan Vukovich using the Edit Citation dialog box.

7. Type the remaining text shown in Figure WB-U2.2.

8. Edit the Ivan Vukovich source by changing the last name to *Vulkovich* in the *Master List* section of the Source Manager dialog box. Click Yes at the message asking about updating the source in both the *Master List* and the *Current List* sections.

9. Create a new source in the document using the Source Manager dialog box and include the following source information for a journal article:

Author	Sonia Jaquez
Title	Organizing a Web Page
Journal Name	Design Techniques
Year	2018
Pages	32-44
Volume	9

10. Type the following sentence at the end of the last paragraph in the document: Browsers look for pages with these names first when a specific file at a website is requested, and index pages display by default if no other page is specified.
11. Insert a citation for Sonia Jaquez at the end of the sentence you just typed.
12. Insert a citation for Claudia Mercado following the second sentence in the first paragraph of the document.
13. Insert a works cited page at the end of the document on a separate page.
14. Format the works cited page as follows to meet MLA requirements:
    a. Select the *Works Cited* title and all the entries and then click the *No Spacing* style.
    b. Change the font to Cambria, the font size to 12 points, and the line spacing to double spacing.
    c. Center the title *Works Cited*.
    d. Format the works cited entries with a hanging indent. ***Hint: Use Ctrl + T to create a hanging indent.***
15. Save and then print **U2-DesignWebsite.docx**.
16. Change the document and works cited page from MLA style to APA style. Change the title *Works Cited* to *References* and format the references in the list with 12-point Cambria.
17. Save **U2-DesignWebsite.docx**, print page 3, and then close the document.

Figure WB-U2.2 Assessment 4

One of the first tasks in website development is finding a good host for the site. Essentially, a web host lets you store copies of your web pages on the hard drive of a powerful computer connected to the Internet with a fast connection that can handle thousands of users (Mercado). Hosting your own website is possible but is feasible only if you own an extra computer that can be dedicated to the role of a web server, have a high-speed Internet connection, and feel confident about handling the job of network security and routing (Holmes). Most people's situations do not fit these criteria. Fortunately, several free and fee-based web hosting services are available.

As you plan a website, decide what types of content you will include and then think about how all the pages should link. Most websites consist of a home page that provides the starting point for users entering the site. "Like the top of a pyramid or the table of contents of a book, the home page leads to other web pages via hyperlinks" (Vukovich 26). Most home pages have the default name index.html (or sometimes index.htm).

Assessment

5

Data Files

Create an Index and Table of Contents for a Desktop Publishing Report

1. At a blank document, create the table shown in Figure WB-U2.3 as a concordance file.
2. Save the document and name it **U2-CF**.
3. Print and then close **U2-CF.docx**.
4. Open **DTPDesign.docx** and then save it with the name **U2-DTPDesign**.

message	Message
publication	Publication
Design	Design
design	Design
flyer	Flyer
letterhead	Letterhead
newsletter	Newsletter
intent	Design: intent
audience	Design: audience
layout	Design: layout
thumbnail	Thumbnail
principles	Design: principles
Focus	Design: focus
focus	Design: focus
balance	Design: balance
proportion	Design: proportion
contrast	Design: contrast
directional flow	Design: directional flow
consistency	Design: consistency
color	Design: color
White space	White space
white space	White space
Legibility	Legibility
headline	Headline
Subheads	Subheads
subheads	Subheads

5. Make the following changes to the document:
   a. Apply the Heading 1 style to the title and apply the Heading 2 style to the two headings in the report.
   b. Apply the Minimalist style set.
   c. Mark text for an index using the concordance file **U2-CF.docx**.
   d. Insert the index (choose the Formal format style) at the end of the document on a separate page.
   e. Apply the Heading 1 style to the title of the index.
   f. Insert a section break that begins a new page at the beginning of the title *DESKTOP PUBLISHING DESIGN*.
   g. Move the insertion point to the beginning of the document and then insert the *Automatic Table 1* table of contents.

h. Number the table of contents page with a lowercase roman numeral at the bottom center of the page.

i. Number the other pages in the report with arabic numbers at the bottom centers of the pages. Start the numbering with 1 on the page containing the report title.

j. Insert a page break at the beginning of the heading *Creating Focus*.

6. Update page numbers for the index and the table of contents.

7. Save, print, and then close **U2-DTPDesign.docx**.

Assessment

6

Data Files ▶

Create Captions and Insert a Table of Figures in a Report

1. Open **SoftwareCareers.docx** and then save it with the name **U2-SoftwareCareers**.

2. Click in any cell in the first table and then insert the caption *Table 1 Software Development Careers* so it displays above the table. (Change the paragraph spacing after the caption to 3 points.)

3. Click in any cell in the second table and then insert the caption *Table 2 Application Development Careers*. (Change the paragraph spacing after the caption to 3 points.)

4. Move the insertion point to the beginning of the heading *SOFTWARE DEVELOPMENT CAREERS* and then insert a section break that begins a new page.

5. With the insertion point below the section break, insert a page number at the bottom center of each page and change the starting page number to 1.

6. Move the insertion point to the beginning of the document and then insert the *Automatic Table 1* table of contents.

7. Press Ctrl + Enter to insert a page break.

8. Type Tables, press the Enter key, and then insert a table of figures using the Formal format.

9. Apply the Heading 1 style to the title *Tables*.

10. Move the insertion point to the beginning of the document and then change the numbering format to lowercase roman numerals.

11. Update the entire table of contents.

12. Save, print, and then close **U2-SoftwareCareers.docx**.

Assessment

7

Data Files ▶

Insert Comments and Track Changes in an Online Shopping Report

1. Open **OnlineShop.docx** and then save it with the name **U2-OnlineShop**.

2. Move the insertion point to end of the first paragraph in the report and then insert the comment Include the source where you found this definition.

3. Move the insertion point to the end of the paragraph in the *Online Shopping Venues* section and then insert the comment Include at least two of the most popular online shopping stores.

4. Click the *Display for Review* option box arrow and then click *All Markup* at the drop-down list.

5. Turn on Track Changes and then make the following changes:

   a. Delete the comma and the words *and most are eliminating paper tickets altogether*, which display at the end of the last sentence in the second paragraph. (Do not delete the period that ends the sentence.)

   b. Edit the heading *Advantages of Online Shopping* so it displays as *Online Shopping Advantages*.

  c. Apply bold formatting to the first sentence of each bulleted paragraph on the first page.

  d. Turn off Track Changes.

6. Display the Word Options dialog box with *General* selected and then type Trudy Holmquist as the user name and TH as the user initials. (Make sure you insert a check mark in the *Always use these values regardless of sign in to Office* check box.)

7. Turn on Track Changes and then make the following changes:

  a. Delete the words *the following* in the first paragraph in the *Online Shopping Advantages* section.

  b. Type the following bulleted text between the third and fourth bulleted paragraphs on the second page: Keep thorough records of all transactions.

  c. Turn off Track Changes.

8. Print the document with markups.

9. Display the Word Options dialog box with *General* selected and then change the user name back to the original name and the initials back to the original initials. (Remove the check mark from the *Always use these values regardless of sign in to Office* check box.)

10. Accept all the changes in the document *except* the change deleting the comma and the text *and most are eliminating paper tickets altogether*. (Leave the comments in the document.)

11. Save, print, and then close **U2-OnlineShop.docx**.

Assessment 8

Data Files

Combine Documents

1. Open **Software.docx** and then save it with the name **U2-Software**.
2. Close **U2-Software.docx**.
3. At a blank screen (no document open), combine **U2-Software.docx** (the original document) with **Software-AL.docx** (the revised document) into the original document.
4. Save **U2-Software.docx**.
5. Print the document with markups.
6. Accept all the changes to the document.
7. Make the following changes to the document:

  a. Apply the Basic (Stylish) style set.

  b. Apply the Wisp theme.

  c. Apply the Red theme colors.

  d. Insert the Austin footer.

8. Save, print, and then close **U2-Software.docx**.

Assessment 9

Data Files

Link Excel Data with a Word Document

1. Open **NCUHomeLoans.docx** and then save it with the name **U2-NCUHomeLoans**.
2. Open Excel and then open **NCUMortgages.xlsx**.
3. Save the Excel workbook with the name **U2-NCUMortgages**.
4. Select the range A2:G14 and then link the cells to the end of the **U2-NCUHomeLoans** Word document as a Microsoft Excel Worksheet Object. *Hint: Use the Paste Special dialog box.*
5. Save, print, and then close **U2-NCUHomeLoans.docx**.

6. With Excel active, make the following changes to the data:
   a. Click in cell A3, type 200000, and then press the Enter key.
   b. Click in cell A3 and then use the fill handle to copy the contents of cell A3 down to cells A4 through A6. (This inserts *$200,000* in the cells.)
7. Save and then close **U2-NCUMortgages.xlsx**.
8. Open **U2-NCUHomeLoans.docx** and click Yes at the message asking if you want to update the document.
9. Save, print, and then close **U2-NCUHomeLoans.docx**.

Assessment 10
Restrict Formatting in a Report

Data Files

1. Open **CompPioneers.docx** and then save it with the name **U2-CompPioneers**.
2. Display the Restrict Editing task pane and then restrict formatting to the Heading 1 and Heading 2 styles. (At the message that displays asking if you want to remove formatting or styles that are not allowed, click No.)
3. Enforce the protection and include the password *report*.
4. Click the Available styles hyperlink in the Restrict Editing task pane.
5. Apply the Heading 1 style to the title of the report (*PIONEERS OF COMPUTING*) and apply the Heading 2 style to the two headings in the report (*Konrad Zuse* and *William Hewlett and David Packard*).
6. Close the Styles task pane.
7. Close the Restrict Editing task pane.
8. Save, print, and then close **U2-CompPioneers.docx**.

Assessment 11
Insert Document Properties and Save a Document in a Previous Version of Word

Data Files

1. Open **KLHPlan.docx** and then save it with the name **U2-KLHPlan**.
2. Make the following changes to the document:
   a. Apply the Heading 1 style to the three headings in the document: *Plan Highlights*, *Quality Assessment*, and *Provider Network*.
   b. Change the style set to Centered.
   c. Apply the Blue II theme colors.
3. Move the insertion point to the end of the document and then insert the document **KLHPlanGraphic.docx**.
4. Display the U2-KLHPlan.docx Properties dialog box and then type the following in the specified text boxes:

Title	Key Life Health Plan
Subject	Company Health Plan
Author	(Insert your first and last names.)
Category	Health Plan
Keywords	health, plan, network
Comments	This document describes highlights of the Key Life Health Plan.

5. Close the dialog box.
6. Save the document and then print only the document properties.
7. Inspect the document and remove any hidden text.
8. Save and then print **U2-KLHPlan.docx**.
9. Assume that the document will be read by a colleague with Word 2003. Run the Compatibility Checker to determine what features are not supported by earlier versions of Word.

10. Save the document in the *Word 97-2003 Document (*.doc)* format and name it **U2-KLHPlan-2003format**.
11. Close **U2-KLHPlan-2003format.doc**.

Writing Activities

The following writing activities give you the opportunity to practice your writing skills and demonstrate an understanding of some of the important Word features you have mastered in this unit.

Activity

1

Prepare an APA Guidelines Document

You work for a psychiatric medical facility and many of the psychiatrists and psychiatric nurses you work with submit papers to journals that require formatting in APA style. Your supervisor has asked you to prepare a document that describes the APA guidelines and then provides the steps on how to format a Word document in APA style. Find a website that provides information on APA style and include the hyperlink in your document. (Consider websites for writing labs at colleges and universities.) Apply formatting to enhance the appearance of the document. Save the document and name it **U2-APA**. Print and then close **U2-APA.docx**.

Activity

2

Data Files

Create a Rental Form Template

You work in a real estate management company that manages rental houses. You decide to automate the standard rental form that is normally filled in by hand. Open **LeaseAgreement.docx** and then save the document and name it **U2-LeaseAgreement**. Look at the lease agreement document and determine how to automate it so it can be filled in using the Find and Replace feature in Word. Change the current *Lessor* and *Lessee* names to *LESSOR* and *LESSEE*. Save the document as a template named *LeaseForm* in the Custom Office Templates folder. Open a document based on the **LeaseForm.dotx** template (from the New backstage area) and then find and replace the following text. Use your judgment about which occurrences should be changed and which should not.

DAY	22nd
MONTH	February
YEAR	2018
RENT	$950
DEPOSIT	$500
LESSOR	Samantha Herrera
LESSEE	Daniel Miller

Save the document and name it **U2-Lease1**. Print and then close **U2-Lease1.docx**. Use the **LeaseForm.dotx** template to create another rental document. You determine the text to replace with the standard text. Save the completed rental document and name it **U2-Lease2**. Print and then close **U2-Lease2.docx**.

Internet Research

Create a Job Search Report

Use a search engine to locate companies that offer employment opportunities. Search for companies that offer jobs in a field in which you are interested in working. Locate at least three websites and then create a report in Word that includes the following information about each site:

- Name, address, and URL
- A brief description
- Employment opportunities available

Create a hyperlink from your report to each site and include any additional information pertinent to the site. Apply formatting to enhance the document. Save the document and name it **U2-JobSearch**. Print and then close **U2-JobSearch.docx**.

Job Study

Data Files

Format a Guidelines Report

As a staff member of a computer e-tailer, you are required to maintain cutting-edge technology skills, including being well versed in the use of new software programs, such as those in the Microsoft Office 2016 suite. Recently, your supervisor asked you to develop and distribute a set of strategies for reading technical and computer manuals that staff members will use as they learn new programs. Use the concepts and techniques you learned in this unit to edit the guidelines report as follows:

1. Open **Strategies.docx** and then save it with the name **U2-Strategies**.
2. Turn on Track Changes and then make the following changes:
   a. Change all the occurrences of *computer manuals* to *technical and computer manuals*.
   b. Format the document with appropriate heading styles.
   c. Insert at least two comments about the content and/or formatting of the document.
   d. Print the list of markups.
   e. Accept all the tracked changes.
3. Turn off Track Changes.
4. Insert a table of contents.
5. Number the pages in the document.
6. Create a cover page.
7. Save, print, and then close **U2-Strategies.docx**.